Service Business Costing

Markus B. Baum

Service Business Costing

Cost Accounting Approach for the Service Industry

Foreword by Dr. Kerry Sullivan

Springer Gabler

RESEARCH

Markus B. Baum
Mainz, Germany

MBA Dissertation, University of Surrey, England, 2012

ISBN 978-3-8349-4443-6 ISBN 978-3-8349-4444-3 (eBook)
DOI 10.1007/978-3-8349-4444-3

Library of Congress Control Number: 2012947016

The Deutsche Nationalbibliothek lists this publication in the Deutsche Nationalbibliografie; detailed bibliographic data are available in the Internet at http://dnb.d-nb.de.

Springer Gabler

Printed on acid-free paper

Springer Gabler is a brand of Springer DE. Springer DE is part of Springer Science+Business Media.
www.springer-gabler.de

Foreword

The costs associated with service provision are often problematic especially in areas where there is significant pressure on pricing. With a growing emphasis on outcomes pricing, the need to understand and control the costs that arise is paramount. Service companies often have high overheads and traditional costing methodologies are not providing adequate solutions in an outcomes based environment. In using a value chain analysis approach this thesis offers an insight into a more efficient method of dealing with the real costs of a project.

The core of the content after a brief examination of the traditional costing models relates to the use of value chain analysis in providing a systemic evaluation for the allocation of costs as applied to management consultancy. The result is a proposed hybrid model-costing model for a service business which can enhance practice and provides a potential methodology that is adaptable across other service providers. A clearer understanding of costs is essential today and the process suggested offers a thoughtful route through this important aspect of a service business.

Dr Kerry Sullivan
Surrey University

Acknowledgements

Though only my name appears on the cover of this paper, many people have contributed to its finalisation. I owe my deepest gratitude to everyone who made this work possible. Thank you so much!

First, I would like to express my deepest gratitude to my supervisor (MBA-Programme) Dr Kerry Sullivan of the University of Surrey, Guildford, United Kingdom. Kerry gave me the most freedom possible to develop this study and book with my own ideas and styles. With his thorough experience in corporate finance and in academic research, his guidance and support contributed significantly to this book.

I am also grateful to the board members and my Corporate Finance team members of the firm J&M Management Consulting AG (Mannheim, Germany) for funding and supporting my study and research project.

Most importantly, this work would not have been possible without my wife Sandra who gave me so much encouragement, love and patience, especially when our son and daughter were born. I also owe special thanks to my parents, parents-in-law, my brother and his wife for their support and help.

Special acknowledgement also goes to my new friends Marco Hackstein, Marcel Mehling and Jörg Dickerboom, whom I have come to know through the MBA study at the University of Surrey and from whom I have learned so much. Many thanks for making my studies so valuable and for the exciting and enjoyable experience.
This book is my recently deceased stepfather Fabri dedicated. Thank you that you were my biggest fan.

Markus B. Baum

Brief Contents

Contents

List of Tables

List of Figures

List of Abbreviations

ABC	Activity Based Costing
BDU	Bund Deutscher Unternehmensberater (German Federation of Consultants)
BRAM	Basic Resource Activity Map
CAC	Corporate Activity Center
DAC	Delivery Activity Center
ERM	Entity-relationship-model
ERP	Enterprise Resource Planning
EU	European Union
EVA	Economic Value Added
FEACO	European Federation of Management Consultancies Associations
Fig.	Figure
HR	Human Resources (department)
ICMCI	International Council of Management Consulting Institutes
IGC	International Group of Controlling (Germany)
IT	Information Technology (department)
KPI	Key Performance Indicator
M&A	Merger & Acquisition
MAC	Main Activity Center
MBA	Master of Business Administration
MP	Main Project
PAC	Partner Activity center
RAC	Resort Activity center
ROI	Return of Investment
SAC	Sub Activity center
SBC	Service Business Costing
SME	Short and Medium Sized Enterprises
SP	Sub Project
Tab.	Table

VC	Value Chain
VCA	Value Chain Analysis
VCAPM	Value Chain Analysis Process Map

1 Introduction

The global economic system is divided into the primary sector (agriculture), secondary sector (industry sector) and tertiary sector (services). This last sector especially has experienced a significant change in the past and continues to grow.

The trend towards a knowledge and service economy is now ubiquitous across Europe and represents more than 70% of all economic activities and is responsible for the same fraction of jobs as well (EU 2010). In spite of the importance of this sector, in the educational world and common literature this sector is not given as much attention as it deserves in terms of the research in and development of approaches for this sector (Ringlstetter et al. 2004, Mowen and Hansen 2011). This study deals with one of the sub problems for a service company from the financial perspective.

A service company provides and offers services. Services are products (task or activities) that require direct contact between seller and buyer (Henschel 1992). The products are performed for the customer or something that a customer uses (Mowen and Hansen 2011). The differences when compared with classical products are the immateriality (intangible, not storable, not transportable), integration of the external factor (interaction with and dependence on the client) and individuality (Raiborn and Kinney 2009, Mowen and Hansen 2011). Services can also be delineated according to the type of services, i.e. commercial services (e.g. business or financial) and non-commercial (e.g. health service, education). A further classification is low-contact (e.g. online banking) or high-contact. Typical expenses for service companies include the costs for motivation and preparedness. These costs are incurred independent of the use of the service, and are required for an effective program and process planning (Dreyer 2003).

Within the services sector, companies are divided into knowledge-intensive and other service providers. Knowledge-intensive service providers include law firms, accounting firms, advertising agencies, investment banks, management and IT consultancy, recruitment agencies, insurance brokers and engineers (Scott 1998) (see Fig. 1.1).

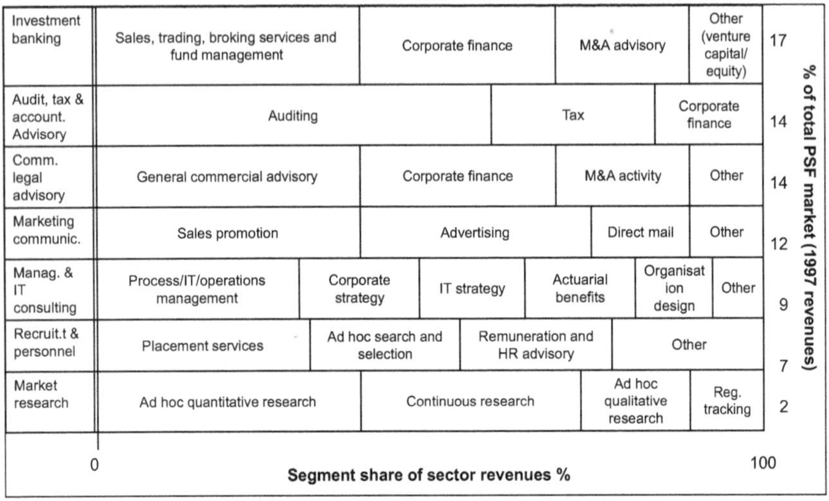

Fig. 1.1 Professional service firms by industries adapted from Scott (1998)

The target group for this study is management and IT consulting firms. Consulting firms, also called professional service firms (PSF), are usually involved in finding solutions to different problems. The participation of the customer is always required and depends heavily on the type of consulting services.

In recent years, the high economic pressure on both the cost and revenue sides have changed the consulting firm leaders' focus from pure partnership-run companies to so-called "managed professional business " (Cooper et al. 1996). Key factors for success in the consulting business include highly-qualified employees with good relationship skills and a good reputation. The company's employees are carriers of knowledge (Shapero 1985) and, as an interaction partner with the client, responsible for company's reputation and therewith are responsible for the future long-term success of the company (Pfeffer 1994). The customers, on the other hand, demand a high level of quality and motivation from the employees of the consulting firm, as they pay for both.

This study deals with the question of to what extent value chain analysis is a suitable instrument for overhead distribution within the development of a cost accounting approach for a consulting firm. The classical value chain originally developed by Michael Porters in 1985 (Porter 1985) is shown in Fig. 1.2 and discussed later within this study. The study is set up as an action research for the consulting firm J&M Management Consulting AG, Mannheim (Germany) and also develops a cost accounting approach for the firm.

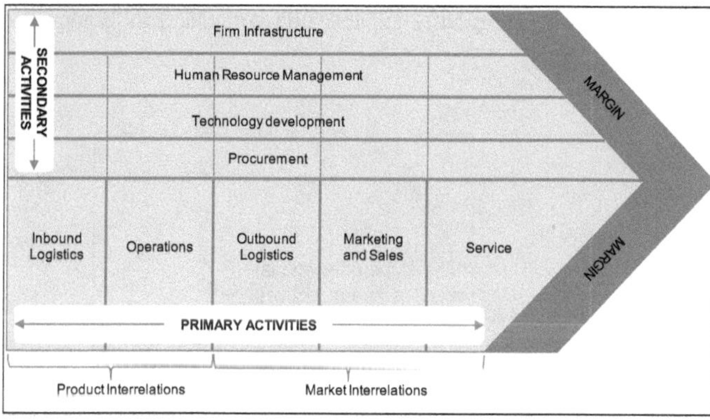

Fig. 1.2 Classical value chain adapted from Porter (1985)

1.1 Target group of the study: management and IT-Consulting firms

1.1.1 Definition and purposes of management consulting

According to the International Council of Management Consulting Institutes (ICMCI) "management consulting is the provision of independent advice and assistance about the process of management to clients with management responsibilities" (ICMCI 2011). There are many other definitions like the one by Fritz Steele (1975) "...any form of providing help on the content, processes, or structure of task or series of task, where the consultant is not actually responsible for doing the task itself but is helping those who are" or with the definition from Larry Greiner and Robert Metzger (1983) as "...advisory service contracted for and provided to organisations by specially trained and qualified persons who assist, in an objective and independent manner, the client organisation to identify, management problems, analyse such problems, recommend solutions to these problems, and help, when requested, in the implementation of solutions" which are just as good. The British institute of Consulting proposes the following definition: "Management consulting involves individuals, whether self-employed or employed, using their knowledge and experience, and their analytical and problem-solving skills, to add value into a wide variety of organisations with a framework of appropriate and relevant professional standards, disciplines and ethics" (Burtonshaw 2010, p. 5). Usually the content of all definitions includes the basic features of transferring knowledge, advice and assistance, independence, temporary service, and consulting as business (Melcher 1982, Kubr 2002, Fink 2009).

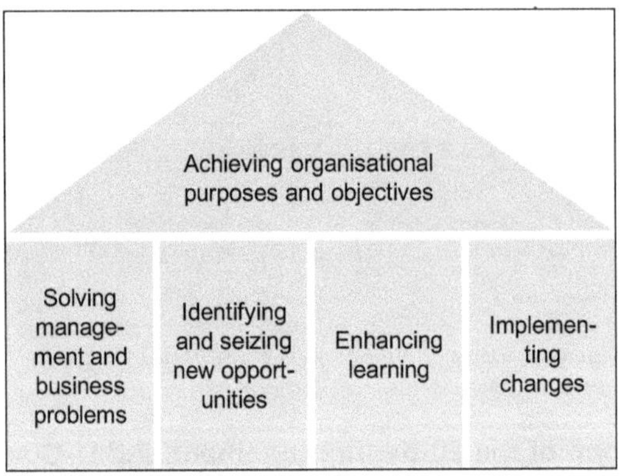

Fig. 1.3 Generic consulting purposes adapted from Kubr (2002)

According to Kubr (2002), consultants are usually used for five broad generic purposes: achieving organisational purposes and objectives, solving management and business problems, identifying and seizing new opportunities, enhancing learning, and implementing changes (see Fig. 1.3).

1.1.2 History of consulting

According to McKenna (1995) and Fink and Knoblach (2003), the consulting industry has progressed through the following historical stages:

1900 – 1930: Initialisation

In the late 19th century, a new industry was developed to meet the need of management in most companies for efficient work organization, and therefore the need for professional help/services (Kubr 2002). This need arose due to the expansion of companies and the rising complexity in work organisation. The first professionals in the industry were consulting engineers, law firms, audit firms and banks, and most often self-employed individuals (Aharoni 1997, Kubr 2002, Fink 2009).

1930 – 1960: Professionalism

In the middle of the world crisis in the 1930s, most companies were out of cash, and control was partly handed over to banks. In 1933, the Glass Steagall Banking Act was passed by the United States Congress. The act forbids economic and organisational consulting through a bank and, for this reason, the demand for specialised external help with restructuring experienced a significant increase (McKenna 1995). The first quality standards for the business were instated (Fink 2009).

1960 – 2000: Internationalisation:

Outside of the USA, the consulting industry remained limited, as most of the business was usually executed through banks (McKenna 1995). In 1960, the first American consultancy firm entered the European Market and introduced the so-called common management methods (Fink 2009). Since

1980, all large and small consulting firms have internationalized their operations. In large firms, those operations count for between 30-70% of the total income (Kubr 2002).

1970 – 2000: Differentiation	By 1970, "strategy" consulting was the main service offered by all consulting companies, and fit to the expansion and orientation of a company's global division. During the economic crisis, this general business decreased and companies began to ask for more individualized knowledge and solutions. The effect was the development of new specialised consulting firms with their own innovative methods and approaches (Aharoni 1997, Fink 2009). The business shifted from general continuous consulting to problem- and project-based consulting with proven standardized analysis methods and individualized solution implementations (Kubr 2002). Audit firms launched IT consulting firms (Poulfelt et al. 2005).
Since 2000: Consolidation	In 2000, due to the economic (dotcom-crisis) downturn, most companies reduced all external spending and decreased their consulting budget, which affected the consulting industry greatly. This financial pressure and pressure from the SEC (American Securities and Exchange Commission) on the audit firms to separate the auditing and consulting business, began the consolidation of the industry. Most audit firms sold their consulting businesses (Poulfelt et al. 2005, Fink 2009) or repositioned them (Nolan and Bennigson 2005).

Since 2005: Revitalisation	From 2005 until the sales collapse during the finance and economic crisis (2007-2009), the industry was growing again, driven by the globalisation of the global economy.

1.1.3 Consulting market

The European consulting market accounted for 83,7 billion € turnover in 2009 (FEACO 2010) and is segmented along the following service lines (see Fig. 1.4):

1. Business Consulting (42%)
2. IT Consulting (14%)
3. Development and Integration (21%)
4. Outsourcing (17%)
5. Other Services (6%)

(Based on the total turnover in 2008: €86.2 bn)

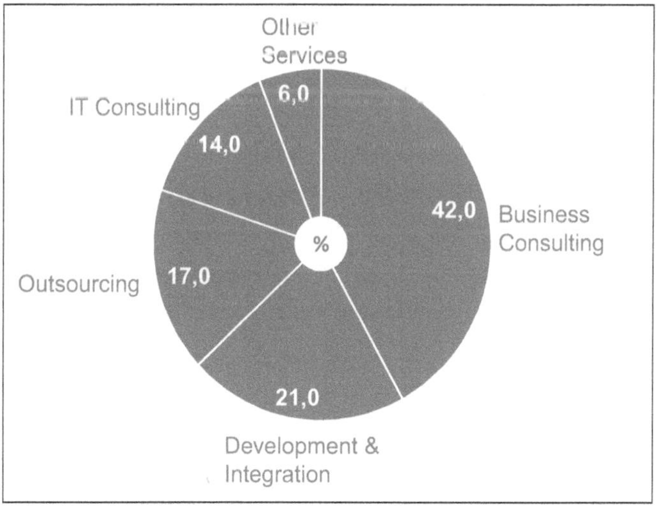

Fig. 1.4 Segmentation of the consulting market adapted from FEACO (2009)

Germany, followed by the United Kingdom, Spain and France are the largest consulting markets (see Fig.1.5).

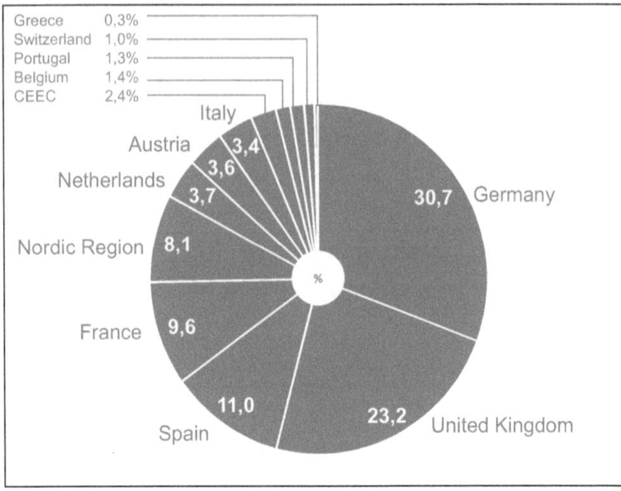

Fig. 1.5 Consulting market in Europe adapted from FEACO (2009)

In 2008, the highest turnover was seen in the banking and insurance (30,7%) industry, followed by the manufacturing industry (23,2%) and the public sector (11,0%) (see Fig. 1.6).

Information concerning daily fees is difficult to obtain from the literature. According to the FEACO (2009), the average daily fee in Germany was 1.600, - € in 2008 (Greece 450, - €, Finland 900, - €, France 1.500, - €). According to BDU fee study from 2008, the daily fee depends on the size of the consulting firm and the level of the consultant. Consultants' daily fees are, on average, between 1.100, - and 1.380, - €. Those of Senior Consultants, on the other hand, are between 1.520, - € and 2.000 € on average.

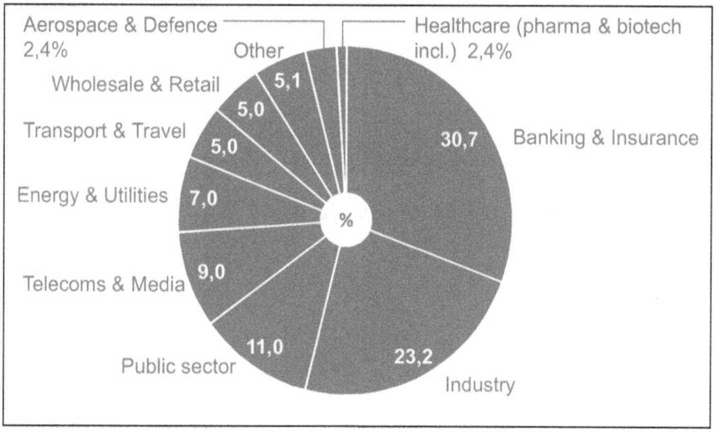

Fig. 1.6 Consulting market segmentation adapted from FEACO (2009)

1.1.4 Purpose statement

In the past, consulting firms were usually able to sell their services on a daily fee with high utilizations and it was fairly easy to understand, without a complex controlling model, if the contract would be profitable or not. The contracts were usually service contracts without any obligations for success or specific guarantees (Stolorz and Fohmann 2005).

Today, customers are asking for more flexible pricing models (e.g. fixed price, value based), more flexible time models (e.g. 2 days a week), more individually specific know-how (rather than just general advice), and for new industry knowledge like public services. These contracts, in addition to the classical service variety, are often contracts for work labour, which include obligations for a certain level of success and quality guarantees.

The conditions in the consulting industry have completely changed over the past decade. To remain profitable in the industry, the management in the consulting firms must adjust themselves to the changes. The current challenges in the industry are discussed in the following section through the use of Porter's 5 Forces model. Michael Porter's Five Forces model describes the dynamics of competitive rivalry within an industry. It is a powerful tool for illustrating the current issues in a business environment. The Fig. 1.7 below shows the set of players that drive the industries and affect their profitability (Porter 2008).

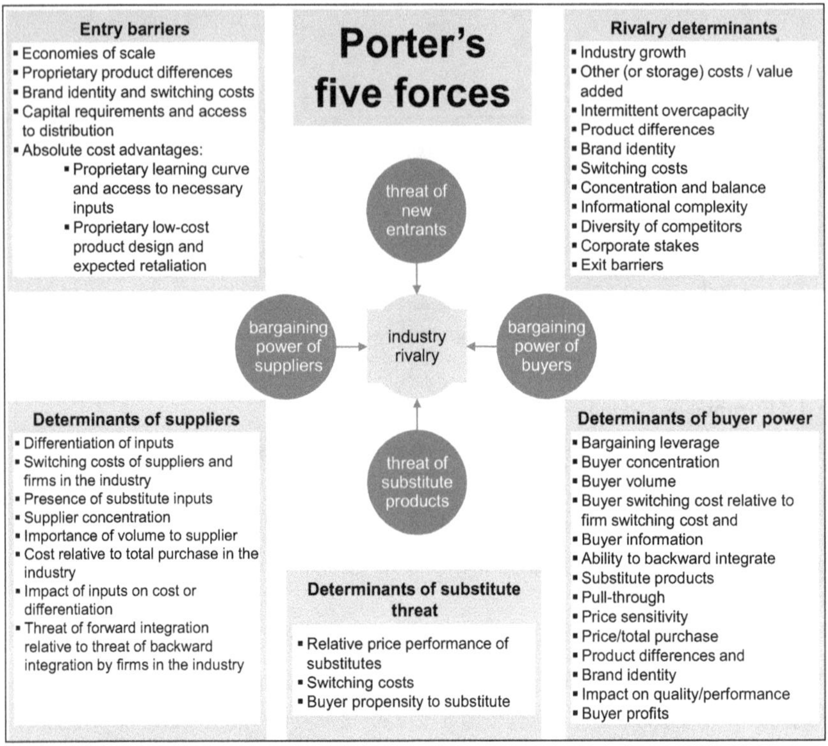

Fig. 1.7 The five competitive forces (extended) adapted from Porter (2008)

Rivalry among existing competitors (in the industry)

Within an industry, companies compete with other companies for market share. The greater the number of competitors in the industry, the smaller the power of the individual company, especially when all companies offer basically equal products and services. In such a situation, a customer will quickly change if he or she is unhappy with the provided package. The topics and industry expertise of the participants increasingly expand and are highly dependent on the current economic position of the customer (e.g. in stagnation, recession or growth). In order to differentiate themselves from the competition, consulting companies have (Ringlstetter and

Bürger 2003) three development strategies: diversification (extending the previous offer), internationalization (wider range of customers) (Glückler 2005) and strengthening the core business (service excellence = knowledge leadership or client leadership).

In Germany (Europe's major consulting industry), the 60 largest consulting firms out of 13.260 (2009) in total, are responsible for almost half of the industry turnover (BDU 2010). Over the long term, the industry is steadily increasing and therefore attractive for the market participant. Also, the new developing markets abroad like India and China should not be underestimated.

The five major services in the industry are IT-consulting, strategy and organization consulting, marketing consulting, operation management consulting and human resource consulting (Greiner and Poulfelt 2005). Each service creates an opportunity for rivalry among existing competitors in the industry, therefore presenting an opportunity to differentiate themselves from the competition.

As the level of competition is high, consulting firms invest in marketing instruments to differentiate themselves within the market. Such instruments include brand building, advertising, dedicated sales force, innovative contracts, books (by or featuring) famous specialists, seminars, and conferences (Poulfelt et al. 2005). A high level of brand identity can make a particular company a preferred choice. As the fixed costs in general are high, optimal utilisation also remains a central goal in the industry.

Threats of new entrants (new companies)

Potential new entrants in the industry may gain their own market share from the existing companies, thereby affecting existing companies' own power. If the entrance barrier in an industry is relatively low, new companies can enter quickly and attack the existing positions. The costs and time in such situations are usually low.

The entrance barrier in the consulting industry is very low as compared to those for lawyers or tax advisers as no legal entry restrictions exist, and the exit barriers are low as well. With this absence of statutory requirements, everybody is free to enter the industry without special experience, education or competence (Poulfelt et al. 2005, Bloch 1999, Burtonshaw 2010). In addition, there are also no restrictions on the use of titles like “management consultant” or “industry leader” etc..

The initial investment to set up consulting firms is very low and an optimal business size for success doesn't exist. The number of players in the industry increases annually. While brand identity is important for further growth, no barrier exists for simply entering the market. The opportunity for customers to change to new entrants is always there, as these switching costs are low.

Bargaining power of buyers (customer)

In an industry with high number of suppliers, the power of the buyer is high. If the switching cost to other competitors is low, as there are many which offer equivalent products and services, it is simply up to the buyers to drive prices down.

The revenue and income of consulting firms comes to nearly 99% from clients in the public and private sector. The volume of buyers is high, as well as the number of service providers. Switching costs for buyers are low and have, therefore, a high influence on the structure of the contract. Recently customers have been asking for more flexible pricing concepts.

According to the Lüdendonk study from 2010, the following pricing approaches are used in the industry:

TOP 1	time and material pricing
TOP 2	fixed pricing
TOP 3	fixed pricing + value-based pricing compensation
TOP 4	value-based pricing
TOP 5	performance pricing (bonus-malus-system)

(Lünendonk 2010).

In time and material pricing approaches, the customer pays a fee on an hourly or daily basis, plus expenses. In fixed-price approaches, customer and consultant agree a specific service (delivery) for a fixed amount. In value-based pricing, the fee depends on the development of another defined variable (e.g. stock, turnover, savings, etc.). Those pricing concepts, like sharing profits in the future or pricing based on savings created in the future, could be, in the opinion of Duboff (2005), highly problematic as "they alter the consultant-client relationship by threatening the independence, if not objectivity, of the consultants" (Duboff 2005, p. 50). Within the SME sector, such contract approaches would help the sector as they often require consultancy for further development but are reluctant to pay for it. Duboff suggests that a value-based pricing concept based on the value a consultant's work has created (Duboff 2005) would be better. In bonus malus approaches, a measurement point (e.g. total volume of consulting days) is fixed; the bonus or malus depends on the target achievement.

In times of low utilization, customers have the opportunity to force prices down, as each consulting company will try to achieve high utilization (Scott 1998). In niche areas, this strategy does not work.

Substitute products like in-house consulting are always an alternative and strengthen the position of buyers, as they are able to do the service by themselves. As enough literature and information about ordering consulting services exists (Munchus 1989, Shenson 1990, Dawes et al. 1992, Patterson 1995), professional buyers are always informed about price sensitivity and the current market situation. They usually use automatic bid systems to achieve maximum value for themselves (e.g. lowest price) by setting quality and performance standards as the requirements for consulting firms to participate in the bid. The normal cycle of how a client usually selects a consulting firm includes: gathering recommendations about consulting firms, contacting consulting firms about general information and experience, description of the problem to a short-list of consulting firms, first meeting and request for proposal. The Fig. 1.8 shows such a cycle with detailed description.

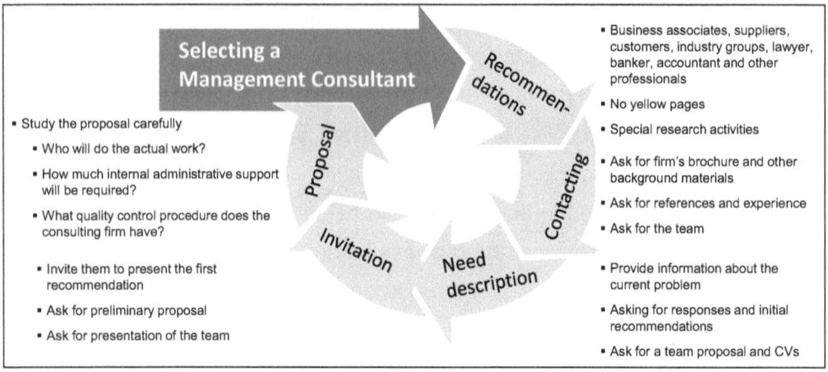

Fig. 1.8 Selecting a management consultant following Munchus (1989)

Threat of substitute products remains

The product or service may be replaced by others. The company's power is affected if the customer finds an alternative to their products and services.

Potential customers of consulting firms are usually presented with the "make-or-buy" decision. A make-or-buy decision is a "decision concerning whether to make needed goods internally or purchase them from outside sources" (Lanen et al. 2008, p. 112). Therefore, substitutes for consulting firms are the rival companies themselves and the growing area of in-house consulting. These consultants have the advantage of already knowing the internal politics, and are usually cheaper than externals. On the other hand, they have no independent perspective on the issues. Communities and universities can further help the development of the in-house business (Munchus 1989) or offer their own organisation's substitute products. Other similar professions like tax consultants and auditors are currently developing substitute products like IT consulting and business process outsourcing (Poulfelt et al. 2005). Many high-level consultants are also former politicians and academics (Bloch 1999).

Bargaining power of suppliers

Suppliers are powerful if they provide necessary input to the operation, and if the switching costs are high. If suppliers are large enough or too raw, they may increase costs.

Suppliers in the consulting industry are freelancers or subcontractors and, in a broader sense, the employees. The key success factor is the staff of the company which, through professional recruiting and retention management, must be managed professionally (Pfeffer 1994). In addition, the mix (leverage) of employees within the hierarchy of juniors, middle-level and senior level, must be well balanced, so that projects can be as optimally staffed as possible with an attractive cost and fee structure (Maister 2003). A hierarchical structure is typical for management consulting (see Fig. 1.9).

A freelancer or subcontractor can be seen as an extended workbench, their issues are close to the issues of actual employees in terms of supplier power. The higher the differentiation to the others is, the higher their power. Switching costs are rather high, as recruiting and on-boarding are time and cost heavy. Especially in times of high demand for specialised staff, the "war for talent" is high. A consulting firm should always recruit and incorporate employees closely hooked to the company because, when employees leave, valuable know how is lost.

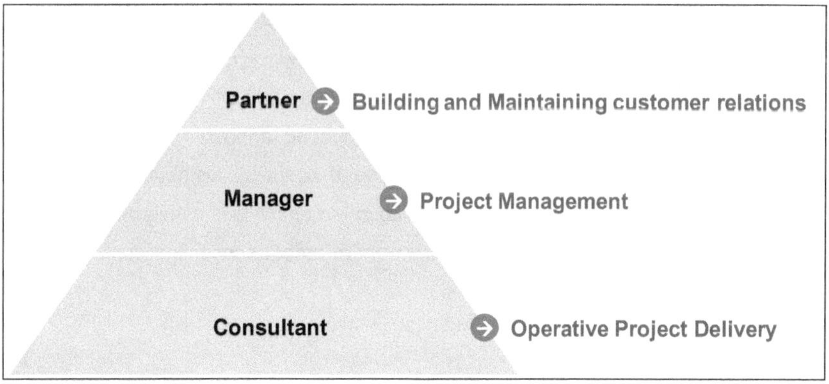

Fig. 1.9 Hierarchical structure and responsibilities in consulting firms

Transfer to the study

To be profitable in such complex areas, it is necessary to understand exactly which functions and operations within the individual organization are value-added, which may not be, and how cost and income can be dedicated to maximizing profit.

Consulting firms need cost approaches that bring transparency to their value chain that helps them find their own improvements.

Service companies (like consultancies) usually have very high overhead costs difficult to assign to individual service products (projects). Costs are often incurred that would be charged to at least two different products (projects). Determining their causes and then distributing them accordingly is always the problem with these costs.

In consulting firms, personnel costs are the highest costs by far. The largest share of personnel costs are fixed costs that arise independently of the sold service (capacity and price) (Reckenfelderbäumer 1998), and, as part of the "standby" costs, are not directly attributable to a sold service (Bertsch 1991).

The consulting firm management needs information about the entire value chain in order to control the company effectively. Having or obtaining transparency for the costs in the value chain and the understanding of how these act or can be influenced is essential. Today the focus, in the service industry as well, lies in maximizing profitability by optimizing operational resources, instead of just turnover maximizing (Kamakura et al. 2002). A cost accounting system can help produce this transparency. The question is, which cost accounting approach is best suited to consulting firms, and how can the high overhead costs be distributed. This study deals with the question of to what extent value chain analysis is a suitable instrument for overhead distribution within the development of a cost accounting approach for a consulting firm.

1.2 Research objectives

The aim of this study is to find an approach for how to obtain cost transparency for a management consultant firm. This study deals with the question of to what extent value chain analysis is a suitable instrument for overhead distribution within the development of a cost accounting approach for a consulting firm. The cost accounting approach best suited to a consulting firm is examined.

The allocation of overhead costs in such a system is essential for a management consultant firm. Using the instrument of value chain analysis, this study analyzes cost-of-division and sets up an appropriate allocation scheme.

The analysis is done using the example of a Management Consulting firm.

The firm is a management consultancy founded in 1997, with headquarters in Mannheim (Germany) and subsidiaries in Switzerland, Belgium, England, France and Russia. The firm combines excellent management consulting with innovative IT consulting along a company's entire value chain. Through optimally-designed business processes and support for modern IT-enabled solutions, its customers achieve their strategic goals more quickly and with lasting success. The firm has first-class professional expertise in supply chain management and related business processes like sales, marketing, finance and controlling. This was confirmed by the hidden champion study in 2009 by Prof Dietmar Fink, which names the firm as the best management consulting for supply chain management. As of 31 December 2011 the firm employed a total of 310 employees in the group. Chairman of the supervisory board is the former prime minister of Baden-Württemberg Prof Dr Lothar Späth. The customers of the firm conglomerates include both international and renowned mid-sized market leaders in the chemical, pharmaceutical, consumer goods, retail, high tech, electronics, telecommunications, machinery and components, building materials, and automotive and supplier industries. The author of this study is responsible for the Financial Shared Service Centre and Corporate Finance based in Mannheim, as the group's Finance Director and member of the Executive Committee.

This study is not intended to describe and discuss the different types of cost accounting systems and value chain approaches in detail, but rather to give an overview of the state of the art and highlight the strengths, weaknesses, opportunities and threats for consulting firms. Models of a cost accounting approach and a value chain analysis will be developed but not monetarily analysed and valued.

This study is not intended to discuss the other success factors or issues in the consulting industry.

1.3 Design of the study

The first part introduces an overview and classification of the service and consulting market. Based on Porter's Five Forces, the problem will be explained and the objective of the work defined.

The second part of the study presents, in a format close to SWOT analysis, the theoretical background and literature review of cost accounting and Value Chain analysis with its different models. Advantages and disadvantages for the consulting industry will be explained, and opportunities and risks identified.

The third part explains the methodological approach, which includes research strategy, research design, data collection and analysis.

In the fourth part, an appropriate allocation model for overhead costs allocation will be developed on the basis of a value chain analysis.

In the fifth part, an appropriate cost centre system is developed.

The sixth part summarizes the findings and gives an outlook for the future and next steps.

2 Theoretical background and literature review

This sections presents, in a manner similar to a SWOT analysis, the theoretical background and literature review of the value chain analysis approach and different cost accounting approaches. For each approach, a brief overview and summary of the approach is provided, which will be discussed in the following paragraphs. The strengths and weaknesses of the approach, and the advantages and disadvantages for the consulting industry, will be also explained.

2.1 The value chain and service value chain

The value chain is, according to the handbook for value chain research by Kaplinsky and Morris (2002) "the full range of activities which are required to bring a product or service from conceptions, through the different phases of production (involving a combination of physical transformation and the input of various producer services), delivery to final consumers, and final disposer after use". Other authors, like Lanen et al. (2008), define the value chain as "the set of activities that transport raw sources into the goods and services end user purchase and consume, and the treatment or disposal of any waste generated by the end user". Mowen and Hansen (2011, p. 27) describes the value chain as "set of activities required to design, develop, produce, market, deliver and provide post-sales service for the product and services sold to the customer." According to Mowen and Hansen (2011), internal value chains exist which also need to be managed. In summary, most definitions contain the transformation of raw resources into goods and services.

The service value chain structures the value processes of a service firm. The traditional value chain framework applies to the throughput of material products while, in the service value chain, the customer is throughput through the process (Bruhn and Georgi 2006). Christensen et al. (2003) argue that customers of service firms are not buying tangible products or even tangible service "products", they are buying a result.

2.2 Value chain analysis

The term "value chain" was originally introduced in Michael Porter's book "Competitive Advantage - Creating and Sustaining Superior Performance" (Porter 1985). The value chain analysis is based on Michael Porter's generic value chain model (Porter 2001), developed in 1985 and used to explore Porter's model of competitive advantages through differentiation or cost leadership strategy. Porter always warns of the danger of being "stuck in the middle" (Porter 1996). The model of competitive advantages will not be discussed in this study as the discussion would be too broad. It should be noted, however, that other authors like Mathur (1988) see exactly this "stuck in the middle" as a possibility for competitive advantage.

Porter breaks companies' value chains down into single activities. The method allows the firm to understand which parts of its operations create value and which do not (Ketchen and Hult 2007). The aim is to cut the entire complicated supply chain of a company into smaller units. Hergert and Morris (1989) state that "the fundamental notion in the value chain analysis is that a product gains value as it passes through the vertical stream of production within the firm. When created value exceeds costs a profit is generated". The model was originally introduced for companies in the manufacturing industry (Armistead and Clark 1993, Ketchen and Hult 2007), which has a significant impact on service firms which will be discussed later. As the Fig. 2.1 shows, the value chain is segmented into primary and support activities.

Primary activities are those involved with a product's physical creation, sales and distribution, and after-sales service. In detail, this involves the product interrelations inbound logistic and operations and the market interrelations outbound logistic, marketing, sales and after-sales service (Ireland et al. 2009, Mowen and Hansen 2011). Primary activities are always defined as value-added activities which are "those that customers perceive as adding utility to the goods or services they purchase" (Lanen et al. 2008, p. 4).

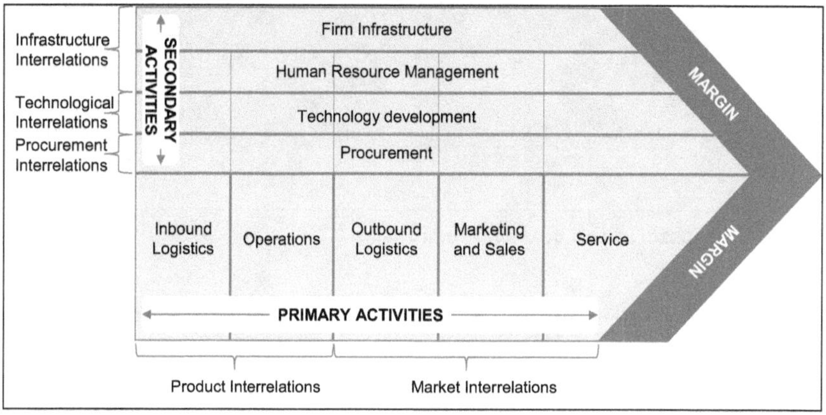

Fig. 2.1 Classical value chain: adapted from Porter (2001)

Support activities provide the assistance necessary for primary activities. In detail, this involves the infrastructure interrelations firm's infrastructure and human resource management, technological interrelations (technology development) and procurement interrelations (procurement) (Ireland et al. 2009, Mowen and Hansen 2011). Those activities are not part of the closer value chain they are included in every function of the value chain (Lanen et al. 2008).

Usually most companies do not produce all components by themselves and has, as incoming, a set of already-finished products. In this situation, the company is part of a larger supply chain (see Fig, 2.2) and needs to consider linkages with external activities (Mowen and Hansen 2011). Porter (1985) also identified the importance of chains or networks which lies outside and controlled by other companies (see Fig. 2.2) (Armistead and Clark 1993). The upstream-suppliers (preceding company) provide input to a company which adds value (own company), which then downstreams the products to the next company (following company) (Normann and Ramirez 1993).

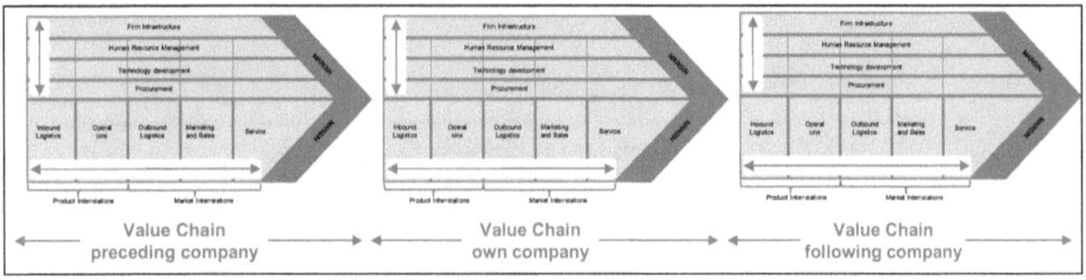

Fig. 2.2 Value chain as part of a network of chains

The target of a well-planned and organized value chain is to maximize value creation while minimizing costs, where all activities of a company link efficiently together (Lynch 2003). The result of adding together the total value and the cost of creating value is, according to Porter (1985), the margin. The total value is referred to as the price a customer is willing to pay (Macmilan and Tampoe 2000). According to Johnson et al. (2008), especially in service organisations, the organisational culture also has an impact on creating value, as culture includes the way people perform the service, which if it successfully enhances competitive advantages and is difficult for competitors to copy.

Accounting data is also essential for the value chain analysis. Therefore, cost accounting is an excellent approach to dedicating cost to single functions and operations (Kinney and Raiborn 2009). According to Lanen et al. (2008), measuring the effects of a value chain is a fundamental service of cost accounting.

2.3 Service profit chain analysis

The service profit chain is an analysis framework that should be more suitable to the service industry than the traditional value chain framework, which was originally developed for the industrial economy. The framework "service profit chain" was developed by the Management Interest Group at the Harvard Business School as a concept for how a service company earns its money (Loveman 1998) and which argues "that revenues are driven by service quality perceptions, which in turn are driven by operational inputs and employee efforts" (Kamakura et al. 2002, p. 296). According to the designer Heskett et al. (1994) "the service-profit chain establishes relationships between profitability, customer loyalty, employee satisfaction, loyalty, and productivity. The links in the chain (which should be regarded as propositions) are as follows: Profit and growth are stimulated primarily by customer loyalty. Loyalty is a direct result of customer satisfaction. Satisfaction is largely influenced by the value of services provided to customers. Value is created by satisfied, loyal, and productive employees. Employee satisfaction, in turn, results primarily from high-quality support services and policies that enable employees to deliver results to customers." (see Fig. 2.3)

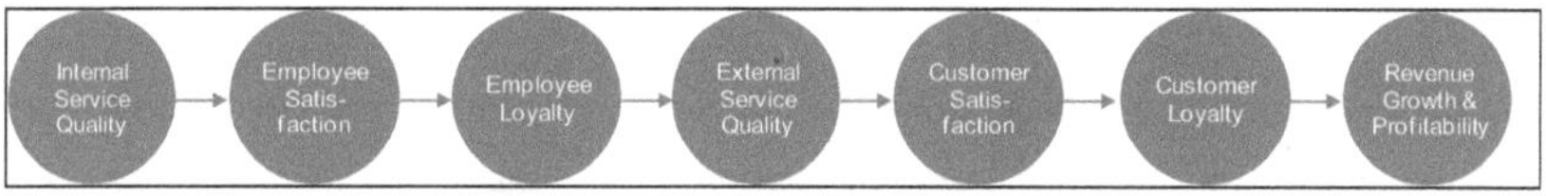

Fig. 2.3 The Service Profit Chain adopted from Loveman (1998)

Simplified, the framework means that profit and growth results from customer loyalty. Customer loyalty comes from customer satisfaction, which is a function of the value delivered to the customer. This function is mathematically represented in Fig. 2.4.

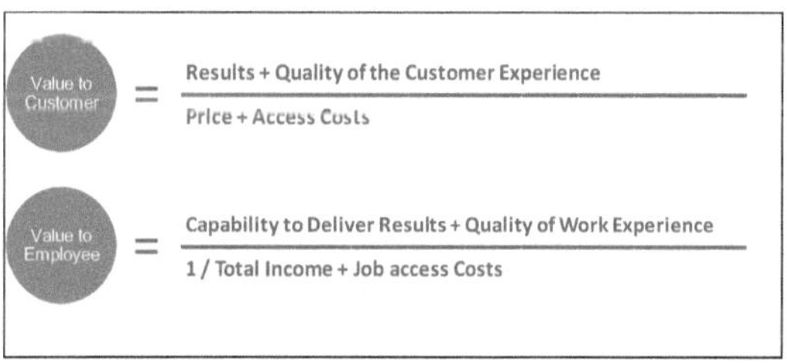

Fig. 2.4 Value to customer and employee formula (Heskett et al. 2010)

The value delivered to the customers is provided by the employee. A high value "delivery" comes from loyal and productive employees, which results, in turn, from a function of satisfaction of the employee, which relates to internal quality (Heskett and Sasser 2010). According to Maister (2001), the quality and customer relationship is driven by the employee's satisfaction. Kamakura et al. (2002) interpret the framework as an integrative tool which translates customer perceptions and behaviours into profits, while understanding the company's investments in the service quality.

The service profit chain itself is a set of elements executed as an operating strategy (Heskett and Sasser 2010). Each activity within the chain has an owner that could be an employee, customer or both. The behaviour and functionality of those owners is essential to understand within the framework. It requires therefore a fully-developed framework of measurement and an analysis of a full representative lifetime of the activities and owner. This analysis could help a firm understand their own strengths and weaknesses.

According to Heskett et al. (2010) the research on the application of the service profit chain framework has not been advanced thus far and needs to be extended. The available data counts for merely insignificant results and is therefore not academically useful. To go forward, better guidance for the collection of data needs to be developed. Therefore, better definition of terms used to describe activities in the service chain, standardised methods of collecting and organizing data, fitting approaches of analysing and sharing those standards with researchers and practitioners is required (Armistead and Clark 1993, Heskett and Sasser 2010).

2.3.1 Strength of the models

Both the value chain analysis and the service value chain analysis are concepts which, through the analysis, could demonstrate the strength and weaknesses of the company and alight to create transparency. The results could then be used for internal and external benchmarking. Internal best practices could be set up within an exchange program implemented in the other departments.

The application of the value chain analysis framework has already been widely discussed in the literature, which includes explanations of the success of various firms (Johnson et al. 2008), basis for resource audits (Johnson et al. 2008), allocations in accounting systems (Hergert and Morris 1989) and as basis for the development of an ABC in service firms (Innes and Mitchell 1990). This makes it easier to adapt the concept for an individual company's purposes and the application is associated with less risk. According to Armistead and Clark (1993), Porter suggests a value chain paradigm in the service industry in a re-formulated model with a focus on cost drivers to gain cost advantages. In this re-formulated model, the primary and supportive activities are divided into steps of the service firm.

2.3.2 Weaknesses of the models

The value chain analysis was originally introduced as a framework for the manufacturing industry homogeneity (Armistead and Clark 1993, Ketchen and Hult 2007). According to Armistead and Clark (1993), Porter recognised originally just the operational flow in a service firm and did not explore the supportive activities. Compared to the manufacturing industry, activities in the service industries are extremely diverse (Evans and Bellamy 1995). Often, no direct relationship between input and output exists, and services cannot be stored. Therefore, a direct application is often impossible and needs to be adjusted to the characteristics of the service industry.

From the perspective that each company is a part of a broader value chain (Armistead and Clark 1993, Normann and Ramirez 1993, Mowen and Hansen, 2011), a strategy could be derived from the concept that the positioning of a company in the right place on the value chain (with right market and products) is the only strategy. Normann and Ramirez (1993) argue such strategies would lead to the limited strategy of placing only value adding activities in the value chain; today, it is also necessary to reinvent value.

The service value chain concept has not been widely discussed in the literature and the application is more theoretically discussed. A broader set of application examples is missing. More research on this concept still needs to be done before the concept could serve as a basis for an application study (Armistead and Clark 1993, Heskett and Sasser 2010).

2.3.3 Opportunities and threats for consulting firms

Value chain analysis in the consulting industry appears to be under researched, as no papers or literature could be found, which obviously seems to be a gap. For the purpose of collecting activities within a company and their value chain, the value chain analysis frame seems to be a fitting concept for the service industry, which also needs, of course, to be adjusted to it. According to Armistead and Clark (1993), the model is useful also in formulation of service operation strategies. It is always the application, translation and further development of existing concepts that provide the right framework. To set up a cost accounting approach, it's possible to find a fitting general framework in the model.

Both frameworks serve the transparency of companies' processes. Value chain analysis allows for the systematic evaluation of the process and helps to find inferences. On the other hand, it is always important for benchmarking to measure the company with other comparable organisations within the same sector. Such data includes operational data, customer data and financial data (Kamakura et al. 2002). Especially for the consulting industry, the collection of this data will be rather difficult to gather without an independent researcher, as the results are comprised of sensitive strategy data. Unless such data is collected over an extended period of time, the results will be not significant.

Burtonshaw (2010) argues that the value chain model is, at the first glance, not fitting to the consulting industry, as the contractual relationship between client and consultant is satisfied by, for example, the exchange of knowledge for an agreed fee and this concept would not fit to the model. On the other hand, he also argues that, on a more detailed level, the model fits as, in the example of knowledge, sharing of knowledge leads to regular improvements and development of best practice.

The service profit chain framework is more valuable as an analysis tool for analysing soft interrelations, rather than hard interrelations of the value chain. To achieve long-term profitability, a service profit chain audit can help with understanding the drivers. According to Heskett et al. (1994), such an audit comprises drivers relating to profit and growth, customer satisfaction, external service value, employee loyalty, employee satisfaction, internal service quality and leadership. For the cost accounting approach, it is necessary to measure hard facts. The framework for this study seems to not be the best fit at this point in time.

2.4 Introduction to cost accounting

Cost accounting has its origin in the manufacturing industry, therefore most of the approaches and terminology refer to it. For this study, it is always important to consider this fact, as the transfer to the service industry needs to be developed. There are lot of accounting and financial terms used in this study which are important first to understand. To assist the reader in understanding the terms, a description of the important terms is provided in Appendix A of this study.

Cost accounting is a part of internal management accounting and designed for providing information to managers (internal users) to assist them in making decision (Martinson 1994, Lanen et al. 2008). It has the three functions: documentation, information, planning and control, and conflict resolution and decision making (Bertsch 1991, Raiborn and Kinney 2009, Mowen and Hansen 2011) (see Fig. 2.5). It's usually divided into cost element accounting, cost center accounting and cost object accounting. Each system can be distinguished according to the level of allocation in absorption costing accounting and variable costing accounting, and according to the level of time in actual, normal, standard (plan) costing accounting. In summary, cost accounting should measure the cost of the performed products or services. According to Martinson (1994), this function is very important as this information influences decision on pricing, choice of product or service and operating income.

1. Documentation	2. Information, planning and control	3. Conflict resolution and decision making
▪ recording the actual costs incurred in one period (one set price and quantity required) ▪ transferring cost to cost objects ▪ combination of formal and informal recordkeeping	▪ orientation, foundation and control of decisions ▪ cost information and tasks ▪ the information is current or forecasted, quantitative or qualitative; monetary or nonmonetary	▪ argumentation and transparency ▪ information to resolve conflict

Fig. 2.5 The three functions of cost accounting adapted from Bertsch (1991)

Cost accounting is often called “responsibility accounting,” as the system of reporting is usually tailored to the company and, within the system, structured so that costs and incomes are assigned to responsible person within the organisation (Lanen et al. 2008). Those responsible persons are assigned to cost centers, revenue centers, profit centers and investment centers.

Often costs of the cost center are based on management decision (e.g. restructuring of a company) or are incurred through legal requirements (e.g. accounting). Most companies try to manage the cost centers through a dedicated budget, which is not allowed to exceed (budget) (Lanen et al. 2008). According to Lanen et al. (2008), such provisions may lead people to suboptimal behaviour in terms of cost consciousness. Unused budget will not be reported as savings, rather, it will be spent as the cost center responsible person will expect to achieve a lower budget if they request a higher or even same budget next year. The evaluation or performance measurement of cost centers is conducted through the behaviour of the responsible person and the fact that quality of the service will not be considered difficult. Ideally, the performance should be measured also by the input factors / products and output factors / products. The achievement of the company's overall goals is more important than the fulfilment of a budget. In the case of legal costs, it is necessary to be in compliance instead of remaining on budget. The cost center approach also ignores the investment made in the organisation.

Revenue center responsible persons have no responsibility for cost. The achievement of own objectives may have a negative effect on companies' profitability through too much spending to achieve the revenue or by badly pricing (Lanen et al. 2008, Mowen and Hansen 2011).

The profit center concept leads to more cost consciousness behaviour from responsible persons as the profit of the center add financial value to companies' overall performance (Lanen et al. 2008). However, the performance measurement shouldn't be measured just by those financial KPIs. Other KPIs, like quality and the alignment to other company objectives (e.g. growth) also needs, according to Lanen et al. (2008), to be considered. The investment made in the organisation will also not be considered. A profit center therefore shouldn't be completely independent in terms of controlling and decision making.

The concept of investment centers allows people to think about and decide on the right investments and therefore calculate and plan in terms of ROI and EVA calculations before the investments is made. Otherwise, such a structured procedure could block innovations (Lanen et al. 2008).

The approach of "responsibility accounting" places emphasis on the responsible person, rather than on the performed product or services. According to Martinson (1994), this train of thought refers not to a costing system, but rather to a management accounting system.

Cost Accounting also has its limitations in terms of the interpretation of the gathered data. Blind usage of the data may lead to incorrect decisions as the data usually looks into the past rather than in the future. Only the deep understanding of the data leads to justified actions for the future. The quality of the data depends on the mental and physical activities of the people who source the system. The lack of publicity of the cost accounting versus financial statements leads to a lack of understanding for recording the need quality (Martinson 1994, Kubr 2002). This and the missing uniform procedure make it hard to benchmark systems and quality to each other.

Within the following paragraph the researcher provides an overview of the common, available costing approaches, and a discussion of strength and weaknesses and the opportunities and threats for a consulting firm.

2.5 Absorption costing model

In the absorption costing model (also known as full costing), full costs (fixed/direct and variable/indirect costs) are allocated to cost objects by recording them in the cost element accounting and allocation to cost centers. The allocation treats fixed overhead costs as product cost; all other costs are period costs (Lanen et al. 2008). The absorption costing model is comparable to the traditional income statement and follows the average, or sustainability principle. The allocation is based on average or proportional relationships to the reference object. It contains both product cost and period cost (Raiborn and Kinney 2009).

2.5.1 Strength of the model

The absorption costing model is a good decision for supporting the pricing of products and services without a market price, or in public procurement. This also applies to the calculation of inter-company pricing or to the preparation of external financial statements. As a traditional costing system, the system is useful for the development of product cost definition (Raiborn and Kinney 2009, Mowen and Hansen 2011).

2.5.2 Weaknesses of the model

The absorption costing model cannot provide information on a short-term price floor especially at low or falling utilization or enhancing direct costs. Fixed costs are treated proportionally as additional fixed parts of the calculation which is only valid at only one volume (Raiborn and Kinney 2009, Mowen and Hansen 2011). The true level of profits can be manipulated through the choice of the overhead cost rate and leads to misinterpretation and incorrect decisions with additional orders (Lanen et al. 2008). “Phantom profits or losses” may arise through under-applied (actual figure is more than applied) or over-applied (actual figure is less than applied) overhead. The reasons for this are differences between budgeted and actual costs, the difference between activity levels (Raiborn and Kinney 2009) or the difference between planned and actual performance is higher than the difference between actual and allocated overhead costs. Remer (2005) argues that it is not realistic that fixed costs (overhead cost) are variable and increasing with increasing numbers of variable costs. The questions of which cost really arises for a final product or service could be answered with the approach which neglects the needed consideration of overhead activities.

2.5.3 Opportunities for consulting firms

Within the absorption costing model, all overheads are allocated to the project and therefore covered by the project. In other words, each project has to bear the overheads. Positive project results (after overheads) provide the company with profits. Together, the sum of all project results comprises the total result of the company.

2.5.4 Threats for consulting firms

The proportional allocation of the overheads within the absorption costing model results in an overcharging of the projects. It is sometimes necessary to calculate a project with a low financial margin or on break-even, as a higher non-financial value may be generated or will follow and was therefore the basis for this decision (e.g. strategic project for entrance in a new customer relationship, trainee projects, market displacement etc.). Such strategic decisions are, from the financial point of view, still within a certain margin, but lead to negative results through the allocation of overheads. Those negative results could be misinterpreted and lead to an inaccurate valuation. According to Mowen and Hansen (2011), fair pricing, in terms of large customers, may benefit by being decreased, as high volume decrease overhead is not possible. Through the proportional allocation of the overheads, high volume projects subsidize low volume projects even though smaller frequent orders increase overhead cost through passing through the customer through whole organisational processes (e.g. master data management, invoicing, etc.).

Project managers are usually rated and sometimes paid based on the project result. If negative project results measure negatively against positive results, strategic project decisions like those described above will be not supported by the project managers (stakeholders). At the same time, project managers usually have no influence on these overheads (Lock 2007).

2.6 Variable costing model

In the variable costing model (also known as direct costing), only direct costs and variable overhead costs are allocated to cost objects by recording them in the cost element accounting and allocation to cost centers. The allocation treats fixed overhead costs as period costs. The model follows the principle of causation, where only costs caused by the reference object could be assigned (Raiborn and Kinney 2009, Mowen and Hansen, 2011).

In the variable costing model, purchased sales minus the variable cost of goods represents the product contribution margin. The contribution margin minus variable non-manufacturing expenses represents the total contribution margin available to cover all other period costs (Raiborn and Kinney 2009). The variable costing model is comparable with the contribution margin income statement. On a unit level, the contribution margin is the difference between price and variable costs per unit and represents "the amount available to cover fixed costs and earn profit" (Lanen et al. 2008, p. 53).

+	Sales
-	Variable cost of goods sold
	Product contribution margin
-	Variable nonmanufacturing expenses
	Total contribution margin

Tab. 2.1 Calculation scheme of contribution margin

The direct costing model is a form of the variable costing model and abides by the following principles:

1. Principle of decision-oriented cost: Only costs which arise through a related decision should be costs of the cost object (Coenenberg 1992). The principle doesn't allow for cost averaging and allocation of overheads.
2. Principle of identity: only costs based on the original decision belong together, which is not equal to the cause-effect relationship (Riebel 1990).
3. Principle of formation of cost objects and direct costs: all products or services could be cost objects, direct costs are costs which are timely and consistently able to be allocated exactly to a cost object (Riebel 1985).
4. Principle of definition of a cost object hierarchy: cost objects should be hierarchically related to each other, as a single cost could be interpreted as overhead on another level (Coenenberg 1992).
5. Principle of temporary relativisation: Costs are dedicated to the cost object only over the specified duration (Coenenberg 1992).

6. Principle of implementation of a basic calculation: the traditional clear division of the model of cost element, cost center or cost object is repealed. There is no separation between fixed and overhead costs (Coenenberg 1992).

2.6.1 Strength of the model

The variable costing model does not allocate fixed overheads in favor of not allocating randomly. The model allows managers to understand the real profitability of products before the allocation of fixed costs (Lanen et al. 2008). This supports shorter-term decisions in the determination of gross margins and lower price limits.

The strength of direct costing is in its clear and logical structure for an accounting approach. It covers the real business reality and provides information that matters. Through a logically setup hierarchy, the analyses of the business form creates several possible points of view (Fischer 2000).

2.6.2 Weaknesses of the model

The variable costing model attempts to make medium and long-term specific calculation decisions that do not cover the entire costs of the company. The method also leads to not taking unprofitable products out from the portfolio in a timely manner (Lanen et al. 2008). The questions of which cost really arises for a final product or service couldn't be answered with the approach which neglects the needed consideration of overhead activities. Remer (2005) argues that if the total overheads are higher than the direct costs, the conclusion of the result of the calculation is questionable. As the direct costing approach dispenses with the clefs of period overheads, it makes it impossible to show a period result statement (Fischer 2000, 78).

2.6.3 Opportunities for consulting firms

The variable costing seems to be a well-suited foundation for a lean project result calculation, which shows the project's really valuable contributions to the organisation. All costs controlled by a project manager are considered in the project result. Other costs, like overheads not under the control of the project managers, are not covered in the project result (Lock 2007). This allows the management to measure projects managers' results.

2.6.4 Threats for consulting firms

The overhead costs are completely uncovered in the variable costing model. If those costs are higher than all results of the single projects, the projects could appear profitable, but leave the company making a loss. In hard-fought customer segments, the variable costing model leads to under-pricing and therefore to a waste of resources. The joint responsibility for the total overhead costs can vanish (Stolorz and Fohmann 2005).

2.7 Activity based costing model

The activity based costing model (also known as ABC costing) is an appropriate instrument for providing the management with the necessary information for the value chain. It's usually required whenever changes in strategic situations (competition, individualism, cost saving), changes in information management are needed (strategy oriented, long-term) or the current cost accounting and controlling tools are insufficient (Reckenfelderbäumer 1995). The overall objective is, through active management of the activities, to reduce cost and to improve customer value (Mowen and Hansen 2011). Through transparency of the value chain and the relevant information, the system relates according to Kaplan and Cooper (1998) to efficiencies.

In the ABC model, all costs are accumulated in cost pools (costs to activities) and assigned to products and services (consumption of activities) by using cost drivers. A "cost driver" is an activity or predictor (activity measurer) which, due to a cause-and-effect relationship, drives costs (Martinson 1994, Lanen et al. 2008, Mowen and Hansen 2011). Such cost drivers need to be identified for each individual business unit (activity analysis and cost driver analysis) and should at the lowest level of activity volume- or unit-based. A "cost pool" or activity center is an accumulator of costs on different levels (unit-level, batch-level, product/process-level, organizational level) (Raiborn and Kinney 2009).

According to Martinson (1994), ABC focuses on three points: "the activities being performed in the company, the resources consumed by these activities and the output being generated" (Martinson 1994, p. 20).

Within the ABC model, the activities will also be classified into primary and secondary activities. Primary activities are those which are assigned as final cost objects. Secondary activities are those which are assigned as intermediate cost objects (Mowen and Hansen 2011). This terminology also fits to concept of the value chain analysis.

2.7.1 Strength of the model

In companies with a large product variety and high product complexity, the ABC is useful for reengineering efforts (continuous improvement), as the system provides information about the relationship between activities and cost drivers (Fischer 2000). The system emphasizes tracing over allocation (Mowen and Hansen 2011). Those cost drivers help to understand which activities are value adding and which non value adding. Through pool costing, the additional overhead cost of the company will not spread over all products and therefore not increase the cost of a product not responsible for the allocated overheads. The costs are allocated to the specific products and services (Lanen et al. 2008, Raiborn and Kinney 2009). The system makes it possible to identify factors that cause an activity, asses or identify the activity and evaluate the performance and results achieved (Mowen and Hansen 2011). Service firms with high overhead costs often apply this approach (Eisele 2001) as it shows hidden sources of profitability and wasteful costs.

The strength of the model is its ability to "operate on the premise that it is the activities and process carried out within the organization which adds costs and value to the products and services" (Evans and Bellamy 1995, p. 36). With the model, the block of overheads is allocated to those activities which actually created the block and not based on arbitrary allocations formulas (Mowen and Hansen 2011). Service firms like banks and insurance companies use the model to acquire information about capacity and operational processes (Lanen et al. 2008). Such information is absolutely necessary for the development of operational excellence.

According to a study from Shields (1995), the six original objectives for the implementation of ABC were: better cost information, product cost information, process cost information, improve cost systems, performance measurement and quality time management.

In summary, the benefits of the system are accuracy in terms of object costing, an enhanced basis for decision making and strategic planning and an increased ability to manage the activities of the company (Mowen and Hansen 2011). The model allows managers, through value analysis, to identify which of the activities are value adding and which are not (Mowen and Hansen 2011).

2.7.2 Weaknesses of the model

The implementation of an ABC is very time and cost-intensive and organisational barriers in terms of territorial, hierarchical or corporate culture can often block it (Babad and Balachandran 1993). To overcome those barriers, investment in training and communications is necessary and top management must be involved. According to Kaplan and Anderson (2007) "ABC systems (are) expensive to build, complex to sustain, and difficult to modify". Furthermore, in terms of information technology, a professional ERP system must be available (Mowen and Hansen 2011). The selection and application of different allocation methods could be very complex and requires time and skills to collect the necessary accounting data. Such additional costs need to be considered for the decision of implementation and justified against the benefits (Lanen et al. 2008). The implementation itself shouldn't be only focused on architectural or software design, according to Cooper et al. (1992), it also needs to focus on behavioural and organisational factors involved. According to Shields (1995), in many firms the implementation includes detailed technical instructions and doesn't cover the human issues, which treats the project as technical innovation instead of an administrative innovation.

ABC was traditionally developed for the manufacturing industries for which fundamentals studies and literature exist. For the service industries, such studies are rare or the access to them are difficult (Martinson 1994). The researcher expects that more service firms will use the approach in the future, as consulting firms are currently promoting the implementation. As this knowledge brings competitive advantages to those consultants, access for a wider audience is difficult.

2.7.3 Opportunities for consulting firms

In consulting firms, the overhead cost, and costs which arise from the corporate functions, are usually opaque and intangible. Managing those costs of the "hidden factory" (Miller and Vollmann 1985) is more important than counting. The implementation of an ABC model leads to an understanding of functions and their cost drivers. Choosing the right cost drivers and balancing cost and result is always important. The goal within an implementation should always be minimizing the costs of accumulating, carrying and managing the information (Babad and Balachandran 1993). Within the model, the relationship and connection to the project business can be explained. Continual analyses like driver analysis, activity analysis and performance evaluation for external and internal projects will be possible (Raffish and Turney 1991). These analyses may lead to realistic and cost object-driven allocation approaches to a project's allocation. The model explains the cause of costs and explains the reasons behind the amount of cost incurred. Furthermore, the ABC model leads to transparency and detects improvement possibilities. This forces the management of a consulting firm to consider the drivers that affect their costs (Evans and Bellamy 1995). According to Mowen and Hansen (2011) traditional cost costing systems don't work well for service firms, as timely and relevant information for decision won't be provided. Activity-based costing systems do provide this, making assessments of cost behaviour more possible and an attempt to achieve continuous cost improvements, which is necessary to achieve a long-term competitive advantage (Mowen and Hansen 2011). Project end calculation (assessment of the project) based on ABC could help to find out what was successful and what was not, in order to develop lessons learned out of the project.

Design steps for ABC System
1. Identify, define, and classify activities and key attributes 2. Assign the cost of resources to activities 3. Assign the cost of secondary activities to primary activities 4. Identify cost objects and specify the amount of each activity consumed by specific cost objects 5. Calculate primary activity rates 6. Assign activity costs to cost objects

Fig. 2.6 ABC design steps adapted from Mowen and Hansen (2011)

According to Mowen and Hansen (2011), a further benefit of ABC is fair pricing. Compared to full costing, smaller frequent order are charged proportionally higher with overheads as large projects, as larger and less frequent orders creates savings. This may lead to price corrections, in terms of large customer benefits by decreases (Mowen and Hansen 2011). Fig. 2.6 shows a recommended process for designing an ABC system.

2.7.4 Threats for consulting firms

For the project part of the value chain of a consulting firm (delivery), the ABC model seems to not be fitting, as each project has other frameworks and solutions. The model would need to be set up for each project anew, and therefore makes for a complex and expensive system (Kaplan and Anderson 2007). As this is a no-go result no further discussions are necessary.

2.8 Job order costing model

In a job order costing model, all costs are assigned to a job, which is a single unit / product (cost object) dedicated to a specific customer (Lanen et al. 2008). A job always has a start and end point in time (Martinson 1994). The valuation of the cost can be based on actual costs (actual direct material, actual direct labour, actual overhead assigned to job at the end of period), normal costs (actual direct material, actual direct labour, overhead applied using predetermined rate at completion of job or end of period) and standard costs (standard direct material, standard direct labour, predetermined rate when goods are completed or at end of period). Overheads are also assigned to a job and the total assigned costs represent the work in progress of the job (Martinson 1994). Costs are applied to the jobs through primary documents like material requisition forms and employee time sheets (job cost sheet) (Lanen et al. 2008, Raiborn and Kinney 2009).

2.8.1 Strength of the model

The job order costing model allows for the tracing of costs and performance for specific jobs and helps to estimate the costs of future jobs (Mowen and Hansen 2011). The model is a useful system for contracts on a cost-plus basis, as all costs are dedicated correctly to the job. The result of each single job could be compared to each other and show the profitable and non-profitable jobs.

2.8.2 Weaknesses of the model

The job order costing model requires the tracking of job costs more accurately and timely than other systems and therefore costs time. The quality of the tracking needs to be very high to get valid results. Usually the model requires a subsidiary ledger account that records exactly the financial transactions and overhead allocation based on predetermined rates (Lanen et al. 2008). Expected income based on the stage of the job will be not considered until the end of the job. The approach only counts costs, and the total of the cost represents the job values as work in progress. Therefore, before the end of the job, the approach gives no information about the ongoing profitability.

2.8.3 Opportunities and threats for consulting firms

The job order costing model seems to be a good fit, as all job (project) relevant costs are allocated to the project. Some public accounting firms using the job costing model as cost accounting system (Lanen et al. 2008). The disadvantage of the job order costing model appears in the need to allocate accurate costs to the project. The allocation of a fixed estimated and appointed cost-rate is not possible. Job order costing seems to be a good fit, if a client (not a project) is referred to as a job. As job order costing only counts the cost, the stage of completion will not be considered. Charging the wrong jobs on behalf of other jobs, for the reason that one job is in danger, leads to misrepresenting the costs of jobs and leads to wrong assumptions (Lanen et al. 2008).

2.9 Process costing model

The process costing model is usually assigned to manufacturing companies with large homogeneous products. The model is an alternative to job order costing, which uses either the weighted average or first-in, first-out method to compute equivalent units of production (Raiborn and Kinney 2009, Mowen and Hansen 2011). In summary, the process costing model, compared to the job costing model (see Fig. 2.7), does not separate costs for each single unit (Lanen et al. 2008), it compares cost for each manufacturing process (Mowen and Hansen 2011). Overhead cost per unit will be usually calculated by the number of performed products (Martinson 1994). As the model does not fit to the service industry with intangible products, it is just listed for reasons of completeness and therefore not further discussed.

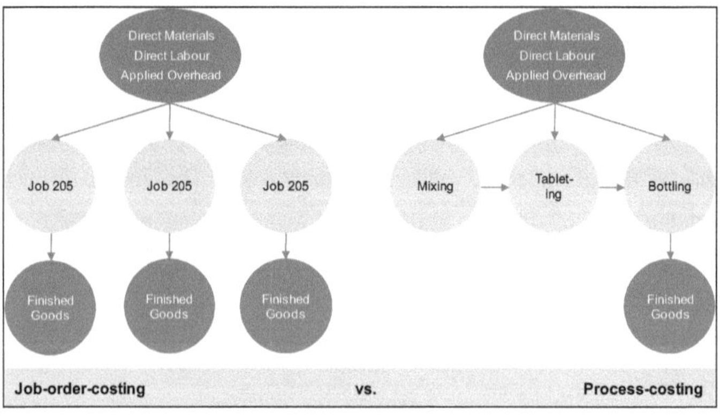

Fig. 2.7 Job-order vs. process costing (adapted Mowen and Hansen 2011)

2.10 Target costing model

The target costing model is a market-oriented model and is a configuration of the product/service based on the possible achievable price. The concept behind it is of "price-based-costing" instead of "cost-based pricing". The concept is useful for calculating a target price by considering target cost. The target price is the price based on customers' perceived value for product and the price that competitors charge (Lanen et al. 2008, Mowen and Hansen 2011). The model "encourages managers to assess the overall cost impact of product designs over the products life cycle" (Mowen and Hansen 2011, p. 7). As this study focuses on actual costing models, this model is just listed for reasons of completeness and therefore not further discussed.

3 Methodology

3.1 Research strategy

The research strategy consists of the selection of the research design and the systematic plan of required actions. The strategy involves making a decision regarding the method of data collection and analysis (Creswell 2009) and must fit to the research study.

The literature, in general, differentiates strategies in qualitative research and quantitative research methods, some studies tend to be both (mixed methods research). Qualitative research takes an inductive approach, where theory is generated from the research. Quantitative research takes a deductive approach, where research is used to test the theory (Newman and Benz 1998, Bryman and Bell 2007, Saunders et al. 2009).

According to Bryman and Bell (2007) “quantitative research can be constructed as a research strategy that emphasizes quantification in the collection and analysis of data” and “by contrast, qualitative research can be construed as a research strategy that usually emphasizes words rather than quantification in the collection and analysis of data” (Bryman and Bell 2007, p. 28). Saunders, Lewis and Thornhill (2009) argue that, in reality, research questions rarely fall neatly into only one philosophical domain (see Fig. 3.1).

Quantitative approaches garner knowledge from post positivist assumptions, where the inquiry strategy has experimental or quasiexperimental design. The methods are predetermined and use closed-ended questions, performance, attitude, observations and census data. The analysis is statistical in nature. Quantitative approaches are used in the practices for testing or verifying theories or explanations, identifying variables to study, evaluating variables in questions or hypotheses, using standards of validity and reliability, observing and measuring information numerically, using unbiased approaches and employing statistical procedures (Bryman and Bell 2007, Creswell 2009, Saunders et al. 2009).

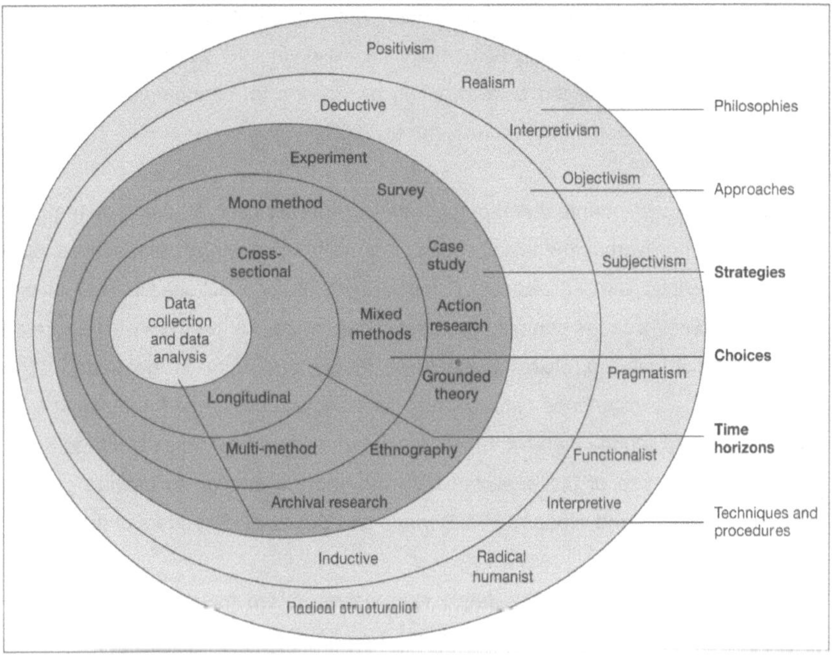

Fig. 3.1 The research “onion” (© Saunders et al. 2008)

The advantage of quantitative approaches is in the collection of a high volume of data and when it uses a statistically valid random sample, the results can be generalised and provide reliable statements. Disadvantages are the limited ability to check answers or to dig deeper for details. Furthermore the cost of research may be very high and people may answer in a way which doesn’t apply to and falsifies the study (Gomm and Woods 1993, Bryman and Bell 2007, Saunders et al. 2009).

Qualitative approaches claim knowledge through constructivist assumptions or advocacy/participatory assumptions. The inquiry strategy for constructivist assumptions has an ethnographic design. The methods are emerging, open-ended questions, field observation, document data, text and image analysis. The inquiry strategy for advocacy/participatory assumptions has a narrative design. The methods are open-ended interview and audiovisual data, as well as text and image analysis. Qualitative approaches are used in the practices for collecting participant opinions, focusing on a single concept or phenomenon, bringing personal values to the study, studying the context or setting of participants, validating the accuracy of findings, making interpretations of the data, creating an agenda for change/reform (Bryman and Bell 2007, Creswell 2009, Saunders et al. 2009).

The advantages of quantitative approaches are the attention to detail in terms of verbal and non-verbal behaviour and therewith portraying perspectives and conveying feelings and experiences. Through the flexibility of actions within situations and times complex cases can also be reliably generated. As the theory is generated from empirical data, a close fit between theory and data is generated. The researcher's own experience can advance the work and challenge the quality of the study by recognizing the disadvantages. It has been argued as a disadvantage of the method that the size of the analyzed data may not be enough to provide general statements (Gomm and Woods 1993, Bryman and Bell 2007, Saunders et al. 2009).

Beside the quantitative and qualitative approaches, mixed methods are always an option. Those approaches claim knowledge from pragmatic assumptions where the inquiry strategy has mixed designs. The methods are both predetermined and continuously developed, both open- and closed -ended questions, multiple forms of data drawing on all possibilities, statistical and text analysis. Qualitative approaches are used in the practices for collecting both quantitative and qualitative data, developing rationale for combining methods, and presenting a visual picture of the procedure in the study, employing the practices of both qualitative and quantitative research (Creswell 2009).

3.2 Research design

This study is set up as an action research study focusing on developing a realizable approach based on common theory. Action research is an approach in which researcher and client, in collaboration, analyze a problem and develop a solution (Bryman and Bell 2007).

Argyris et al. (1985) define action research as experiments based on real problems and then design solutions. The iterative process of problem identification, planning, action and evaluation eventually leads to re-education and changing patterns of thinking. The benefit, when compared to other research methods, is the relationship of academic theory and practical action (Argyris et al. 1985). The outcome and processes should have implications for the real situation and be usable in practices with recognition of the theory. The researcher needs to understand that each finding has implications for the real project and therefore the expectations of the participants need to be clearly understood (Eden and Huxham 1996). The original intent of an action research is to generally effect change rather than meet clear objectives (Stone 1978, Saunders et al. 2009). This means usually an action research project has been set up to change a current situation (e.g. current system) into a new situation (e.g. new system). This means that the objective is less about explaining the current situation.

Compared to a case study, where the research is conducted with a clear situation, the researcher in action research studies is usually a participant in the process, rather than an observer, as in case studies (Benbasat et al. 1987, Saunders et al. 2009). The objectives of action research are twofold: to take action to solve a problem, and to develop a concept for the organization (Checkland 1981). The researcher brings specialised knowledge and improvement techniques into the project and, as part of the team, assists in achieving the aims.

According to Benbasat et al (1987), the strength of an action research study is the in-depth and first hand understanding of the researcher, which conversely could be a weakness in terms of the potential lack of objectivity. However, a further advantage of action research is the output of the research, which is usually more readable, relevant and interesting to practioners than that typically produced for the academic audience. The result of the research is often a discussion document presenting the different opportunities for strategies and recommendations. Fig. 3.2 shows the procedure in action research.

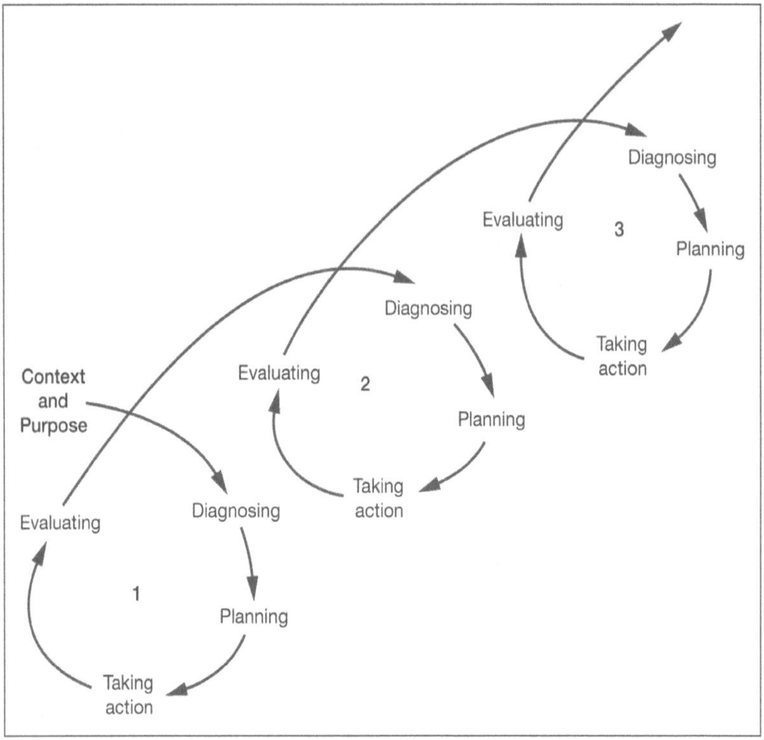

Fig. 3.2 The action research spiral (© Saunders et al. 2008)

The research design should produce the evidence to answer and support the initial question and purposes of the study (De Vaus 2001).

The aim of this study is to find an approach for obtaining cost transparency for a management consultant firm. This study deals with the question of to what extent value chain analysis is a suitable instrument for overhead distribution within the development of a cost accounting approach for a consulting firm. The cost accounting approach best suited to a consulting firm is examined.

The nature of this study is to explore current theory, practice, experiences and perspectives from the people involved with a specific company, concerning the value chain and the cost structure. Through the nature of the study, with its focus on developing a cost accounting system for a specific single management consultant firm and the role of the researcher, who is part of the project, the approach of action research is acceptable.

Action research, like other qualitative methods, is criticized for its lack of repeatability and consequent lack of rigour (Bryman and Bell 2007). Furthermore, an application to other organizations may be difficult for people with less knowledge of how to apply it.

This research analyzes only one firm, but in such a standardised way and based on common literature so that it is at least transferable to other consulting firms. The research is significant as value chain analysis adapted by the service industry is underrepresented (Armistead and Clark 1993, Kamakura et al. 2002, Heskett and Sasser 2010) and, especially for consulting firms, there is an obvious gap in the literature. An approach with strong operational focus may provide missing pieces of research and is essential for service firms. Most traditional costing models neglect the allocation of overheads and only allocate them with a fixed percentage, which does not provide stakeholders with the needed information and leads to incorrect decisions. This study analyzes cost-of-division and sets up an appropriate allocation scheme.

3.3 Data collection and analysis

This data collection section describes the structure and process of collecting information. Action research can involve both quantitative and qualitative data collection. This study only uses qualitative data collection. According to Yin (1984), the following "sources of evidence work well with action research:

1.Documentation:	written material ranging from memoranda to newspaper clippings to formal reports.
2.Archival records:	organization charts, service-, personnel- or financial records.
3.Interviews:	open-ended or focused

4.Direct observation: absorbing and noting details, actions, or subtleties of the field environments

5.Physical artefacts: devices, outputs, tools." (Yin 1984)

This study collects and analyses both primary and secondary data. Secondary data analysis is the analysis of data from other researchers and could involve quantitative and qualitative data. This data has already been collected and is available from other resources. The use of secondary data offers many benefits like cost and time optimization, high-quality data, the opportunity for longitudinal and cross-cultural analysis, and more time for data analysis. Otherwise, it limits the familiarity with the data, the complexity might remain unknown and the researcher has no control over the quality of the data (Bryman and Bell 2007, Saunders et al. 2009).

Primary data analysis is the analysis of data, where the researcher was involved in its collection (Bryman and Bell 2007, Saunders et al. 2009). The advantages and disadvantages are usually the opposite of the secondary data analysis.

The secondary data analysed for this study includes the in-depth study of written material like academic books, journals, newspapers, magazines, internet articles and sources, laws and provisions, and statistics, as well as unpublished data sources. Secondary data also includes internal sources like internal wikipedia, policies, department and activities descriptions, organisation charts, and job description. This approach is beneficial in terms of its low cost and time consumption as existing information are already checked for feasibility. Weaknesses could appear in how up-to-date the information is, which must be checked with the interviews.

This secondary data, structured as a literature review, is the basis and foundation for the theoretical section of this study. The literature review section provides an overview of and discusses the current available cost accounting approaches and value chain analysis, whether it fits to a management consulting firm or not. As already expected, a lot of literature exists but most of them do not refer to the service industry and especially not to the consulting industry. Out of this literature review (data analysis), a cost accounting approach will be developed and discussed.

The primary data in this study is collected in semi-structured interviews. Interviewing is a useful method for collecting data about complex issues that allows the involved parties to explore their personal perspectives and process the interview flexibly (Bryman and Bell 2007, Saunders et al. 2009).

Before the interview, the researcher, using semi-structured interviews, prepared a list with subjects and questions for guiding the interview. This guide was sent to the interviewees before the meeting for preparation. It was necessary to speak in the language of the organisation to communicate the objectives of the study. The researcher contacted the interview partners by email and follow-up calls made sure that the emails were received and the scheduled meetings were possible. All receivers of the email confirmed participation in the study

A good facilitation is necessary to point out pieces of information where more detail is needed. Within the interview, the research is conducted flexibly in order to cover all questions or to go into more detail (Denscombe 2010). According to Rathnow (2011), interviewing employees with the best overview of all process is the recommend procedure for gathering information about processes.

To obtain a cross-sectional view of all value chain participants, interview partners are all leaders of corporate functions, management and samplings of consultants, administration staff, and partners (sampling). The course of action and the data analysis is explained in section 4.1.

3.4 Ethics

Research ethics refers to, according to Saunders et al. 2009, the appropriateness behaviour of the researcher in terms of protecting the rights and privacy of the persons involved in the research including the researchers themselves. In all stages of the research, sensitive and personal data will be collected, analysed and findings reported. It needs to be ensured that no harm comes to any participant. Trochim (2006) provides the following principles:

1. Principle of voluntary participation
2. Principle of informed consent
3. Principle of no risk of harm
4. Principle of confidential and anonymity

The researcher applied the above-mentioned principles and the “Code on Good Research Practice” of the University of Surrey (Guildford, United Kingdom) and confirmed this by completing the appropriate form from the university.

4 Action research: value chain analysis of the firm

4.1 Course of actions

To set up a value chain for the company, and further understand the main issues in the value chain, the researcher follows the following course of action, creating the action research portion of the study.

First (1) an overview of the structure of the company and the specific characteristics of the delivery and corporate functions is given. (2) Thereafter, the standard consulting process is discussed and further developed for the research company. This standard consulting process, at the same time, will be the main process of the company. Based on this, a hypothetical definition of all activities and operations broken down by function, follows. (3) In the next phase, the supporting processes are discussed and hypotheticals are collected for the company. Thereby, the concept of routine and strategic activities will be explained. The hypothetical breakdown of all activities and operations is important for the verification that will follow later. (4) Based on the hypothetical definition and the thereby derived maps of the main processes and supportive processes, the classical value chain concept will be adapted for a service company and an adjustment to the value chain made for the company. All activities and operations are assigned to the traditional categories of primary and support activities. (5) In the fifth phase, the hypothetical definitions and breakdowns will be verified. The verification will be conducted in interviews with the individual department supervisors. The interviews are conducted with the help of previously set-up process maps for each department. At the same time, all cost drivers of the process will be collected for further assignment. (6) In the next phase, the interviews and then hypotheses will be evaluated. The cost drivers in the processes will also be analyzed. In the last phase (7), the results of the study will be interpreted, in which the conditions for the cost accounting system will also be discussed. In this interpretation phase, all activities will be classified into value-adding, routine and strategic activities. Based on the results and classification, a cost allocation approach for each classification should follow. The course of action is also shown in figure Fig. 4.1 below.

1. Introduction and overview of the corporate structure (functions)

- Overview structure of companies functions
- Delivery functions
- Corporate functions

↓

2. Hypothetical definition of main processes

- Introduction main process (consulting process)
- Further development of the consulting process
- Hypothetical definition of main process activities for each function

↓

3. Hypothetical definition of supportive processes

- Introduction to supportive processes
- Concept of routine and strategic activities
- Hypothetical definition of supportive process activities for each function

↓

4. Development of the value chain

- Introduction to value chain analysis in the service industry
- Adapting of the value chain concept to the research firm
- Assignment of the main process and supportive processes to the value chain

↓

5. Verification hypothetical definition

- Introduction to verification
- Verification map / interviews
- Verification of all main and supportive processes

↓

6. Activity and cost driver analysis

- Introduction
- Activity and cost driver analysis of all main and supportive processes
- Verification hypothesis

↓

7. Interpretation and transfer phases

- Classification of the activities and operations in value adding, routine and strategic activities
- Cost allocation approach for value adding, routine and strategic activities
- Requirements of a cost accounting approach

Fig. 4.1 Course of actions

4.2 Definition and development phases

4.2.1 Introduction / overview of the corporate structure (functions)

To set up a compilation of all important main process of the studied company, it is necessary to understand the structure of the company first. The figure below shows the hierarchical composition of the function and shows the typical split (Maister 2001, Kubr 2002) of the functions in a consulting firm into delivery functions and corporate functions (see figure Fig. 4.2).

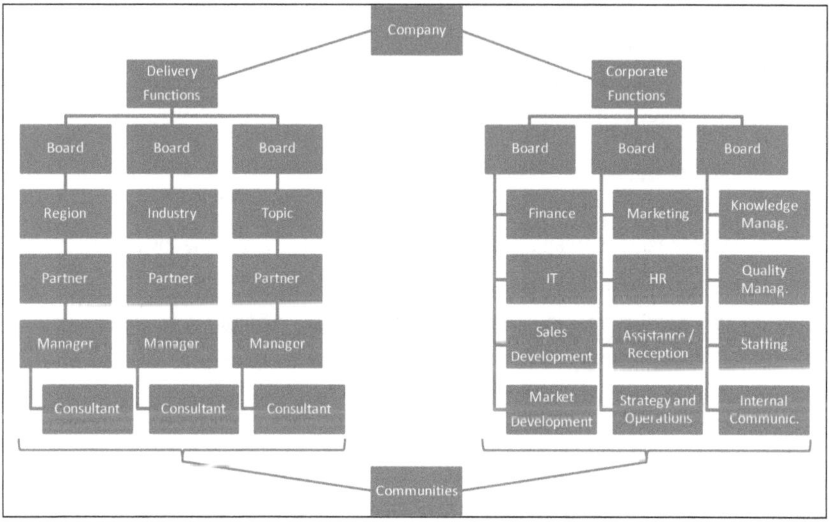

Fig. 4.2 Typical split of a consulting firm

The company has basically two streams of activities and operations (delivery and corporate). Delivery functions are the unit that has the primary contact with the customers. All consultants, who make up the main volume of the employees of the company, are assigned to this stream. Consultants are those employees who work for customers on projects. The highest lead-function of the consultants is partner (a person's title and role), who is part of the management team of the organisation, and dedicated at least to one of the stream's regions, industries or topics. A region is an explicitly defined area of countries for which a partner is responsible. An industry is explicitly defined area of industries and customers for these industries for which a partner is responsible. A topic is an explicitly defined area of solutions for which a partner is responsible. The next hierarchical level is the manager-level, each of whom is dedicated to a partner and usually has dedicated consultants to lead. Within the hierarchical levels of partner and manager, consultants can be further hierarchically classified into associate and senior. The delivery stream is significantly responsible for the achievement of turnover. The higher a consultant is in the hierarchy of the company, the stronger the expectation of the company will be that such consultants are not only responsible for doing their work on the project (in the delivery), but are also responsible for the further development of the company (e.g. method development) and, in terms of turnover growth, being part of the sales team; selling projects. The remuneration system is always aligned to those objectives.

But, the outcome and growth of a consulting firm can't be measured only by the revenue performed by the delivery functions. It is a more complex process that is also at work inside each consulting firm. This work is managed and planned by corporate functions (Greiner and Malernee 2005). Corporate functions are the unit that do not have primary contact with the customers. Employees in corporate functions usually do not work on external projects, but are always involved with or lead internal projects. Corporate functions are a key element of a company's structure and are responsible for corporate policies and corporate services. Corporate policies are all policies (legislation) that are necessary by law (e.g. policies regarding workplace security, equality) or by internal necessity to lead and organize a company. This also involves the vision, mission and values of a company. Corporate services are the execution of the policies and the administration of a company. This involves strategic functions (setting and execution of a strategy), operative functions (setting and execution of a standard process) and routine functions (setting and execution of mass processes). A hierarchy within corporate functions also exists (director, manager, specialist or analyst) and the topic areas are delineated into resorts / departments. In order for a company to perform well, it is always important that all functions work together.

4.2.2 Hypothetical definition of main processes/operations

According to Kubr (2002), the simple consulting process has 5 phases: entry, diagnosis, action planning, implementation and termination (see Fig. 4.3). The literature often refers to the Kolb-Frohman phases as well, which describes them as: scouting, entry, diagnosis, planning, action, evaluation, termination (Kolb and Frohman 1970).

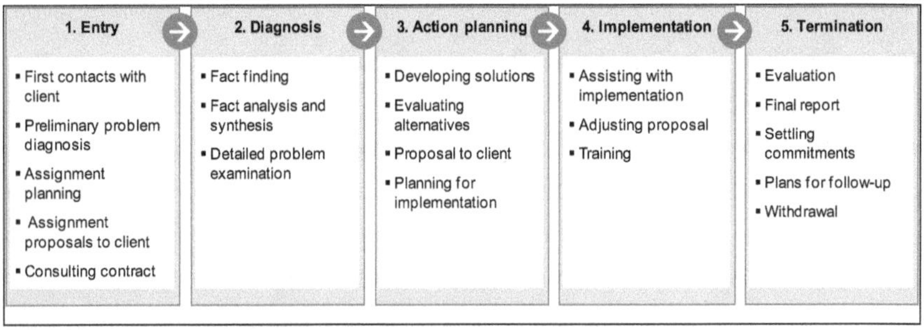

Fig. 4.3 The consulting process adopted from Kubr (2002)

The phases of the consulting process can also be seen as operations. The researcher applies the concept of Kubr (2002) and the Kolb-Frohman model (1970) with enhancements and adjustments. The models of Kubr and Kolb-Frohman can be seen as very delivery-orientated and as under representing the corporate functions. In the opinion of the researcher, before the "entry phases" can be successful, research into the industry, with its companies and market behaviour is necessary. Customer relationship management, marking activities and direct calling are typical activities of the corporate functions in the phases "identify and development". This phase is settled before the phase 1 (entry) in Kubr's model.

In the phase "sell and entry", which is a combination of the phases 1 (entry) and 2 (diagnosis) of Kubr's model, the first contact with the client and the sales cycle, with preliminary problem diagnosis and solution offering within a proposal, takes place. This phase is primarily done by the delivery functions and follows the phases "identify and development". After winning the deal in phases "sales and entry," the next phase is "planning and staffing", in which the next interaction between delivery and corporate functions takes place. In this phase, the corporate function provides existing solutions or methods (knowledge management) and provides a fitting project team (internal or external resources). If people or knowledge are missing, HR is responsible for recruiting and training, therefore this function of the human resource management is a main process. The delivery functions are responsible for choosing existing solutions or methods and planning the project. This phase covers the phase “action planning” of Kubr’s model.

The next phase is the core phase of the main process, the “delivery phase”. This phase is a combination of Kubr’s phases 2 (diagnosis) and 4 (implementation), in which the delivery takes place at the customer. The phase covers analysis, problem examination, solution implementation, project management and change request management, and is usually primarily done by the delivery functions. The following “billing” phase was not found in models discussed in the literature. All projects, in time, budget and quality, are of no account from the financial point of view if the billing hasn’t done. This activity is usually completed by the finance department (corporate functions) and depends on the time recording during the delivery function.

The last phases of the researcher's model is exactly the same as that of Kubr. This phase closes the project with evaluation, reports, settling commitments, plans for follow up, and withdrawal. The researcher's proposed main process for the consulting firm is presented in the Fig. 4.4 below. The further-developed consulting process is shown in the figure below.

The inclusion of all activities of the research company follows the enhanced consulting process. Main activities are those activities that are part of the consulting process. Those activities and operations are always value-adding processes.

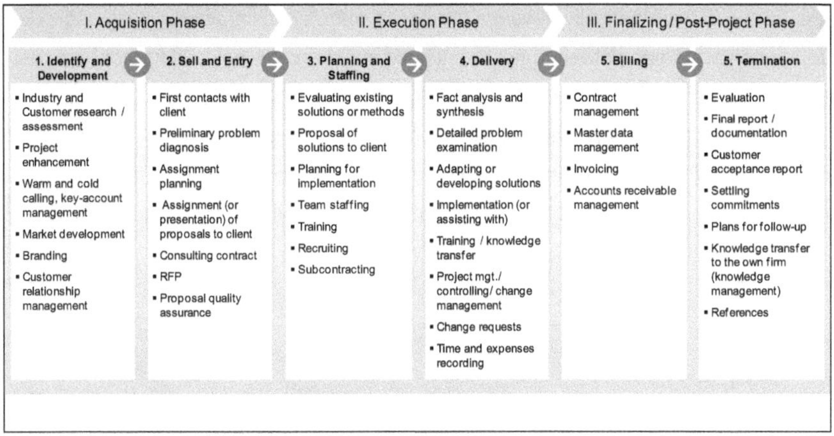

Fig. 4.4 The consulting process extended (enhancements of Kubr (2002))

According to Burtonshaw (2010), value-adding activities occur in three main stages. The first stage is the "pre-contract"-stage (focus on assessment of fit), where "the anticipated consultancy fee multiplied by the value of strategic fit (a value between 0 to 1) less the cost to bid and win the consultancy work" adds value. The second stage is the "project execution"-stage (focus on cost and value), where "value of the overall project multiplied by the strategic value to business less the value of consultancy contract" adds value. And the third stage is the "project completion"–stage (focus on capitalizing the experience), where "consultancy fee multiplied by the value of new work for same client dividend by the time of years" (Burtonshaw 2010, pp. 21-23).

Value adding in the context of the value chain analysis means always activities and operations which are part of the main process. Those activities are by definition value-adding as they are dedicated to fulfilling the customer's requirements (IGC et al. 2011, Mowen and Hansen 2011). Adding value activities through a customer's eyes are activities which refer to the price and the therefore expected added value for the customer. Put the other way around, activities and operations which are not part of the main processes are not defined as value adding (supportive processes). Within the following hypothetically-developed process map, all main activities are dedicated to the corporate and delivery functions. Those maps are the basis of further analysis.

Action research: The hypothetical definition is based on secondary research (internal process documentation of the company, general literature relating to the functions). The overview of activities in the main process by function is summarized in **Fig. 4.5**.

Main Process
(in the function; does not necessarily = value chain activity)

Delivery

- Project enhancement
- Key account mgt.
- First contacts with client
- Preliminary problem diagnosis
- Assignment planning
- Assignment of proposals to client
- Consulting contract
- RFP
- Evaluating existing solutions
- Proposal of solutions to client
- Planning for implementation
- Team staffing
- Training
- Fact analysis and synthesis
- Detailed problem examination
- Adapting or developing solutions
- Assisting with/and implementation
- Training / knowledge transfer to the customer
- Project management / controlling / change management
- Change requests
- Time and expenses recording
- Evaluation
- Final report / documentation
- Customer acceptance report
- Settling commitments
- Plans for follow-up
- Withdrawal
- Knowledge transfer to own firm
- References

1. Finance

- Time and expenses recording
- Project controlling
- Contract management
- Project master data management
- Invoicing
- Accounts receivable management

2. Marketing

- Branding
- CRM
- References
- Direct Marketing

3. HR

- Recruiting
- Training (administrative)

4.&5. Market & Sales Development

- Industry and customer research
- Warm and cold calling
- First contact with clients

7. Assistance / Reception

- Industry and customer research
- Time and expenses recording

8.+9. Knowledge & Quality Management

- Evaluating existing solutions
- Knowledge transfer to own firm
- Training (content)

10. Staffing

- Team staffing
- Subcontracting

12. Communities

- Support for sales and marketing

Fig. 4.5 Overview about main processes by functions

4.2.3 Hypothetical definition of supportive processes/operations

Supportive processes are those activities and operations that support the main process. They are not part of the main process. By definition and in contrast to the main processes, the supportive processes are not value-adding activities and operations, as the customer gets no direct value from them (IGC et al. 2011). This doesn't mean that those activities are not important or that these activities are worthless, those activities are rather routine or strategic activities, instead of value adding.

Strategic activities are those activities and operations that help create (strategy development) or align with (strategy execution) to the company's strategy. Strategy is, according to Porter (1996), "...the creation of a unique and valuable position, involving a different set of activities" it "requires [you] to make trade-offs in competing – to choose what not to do" and "involves creating fit among a company's activities" (Porter 1996, p. 64).

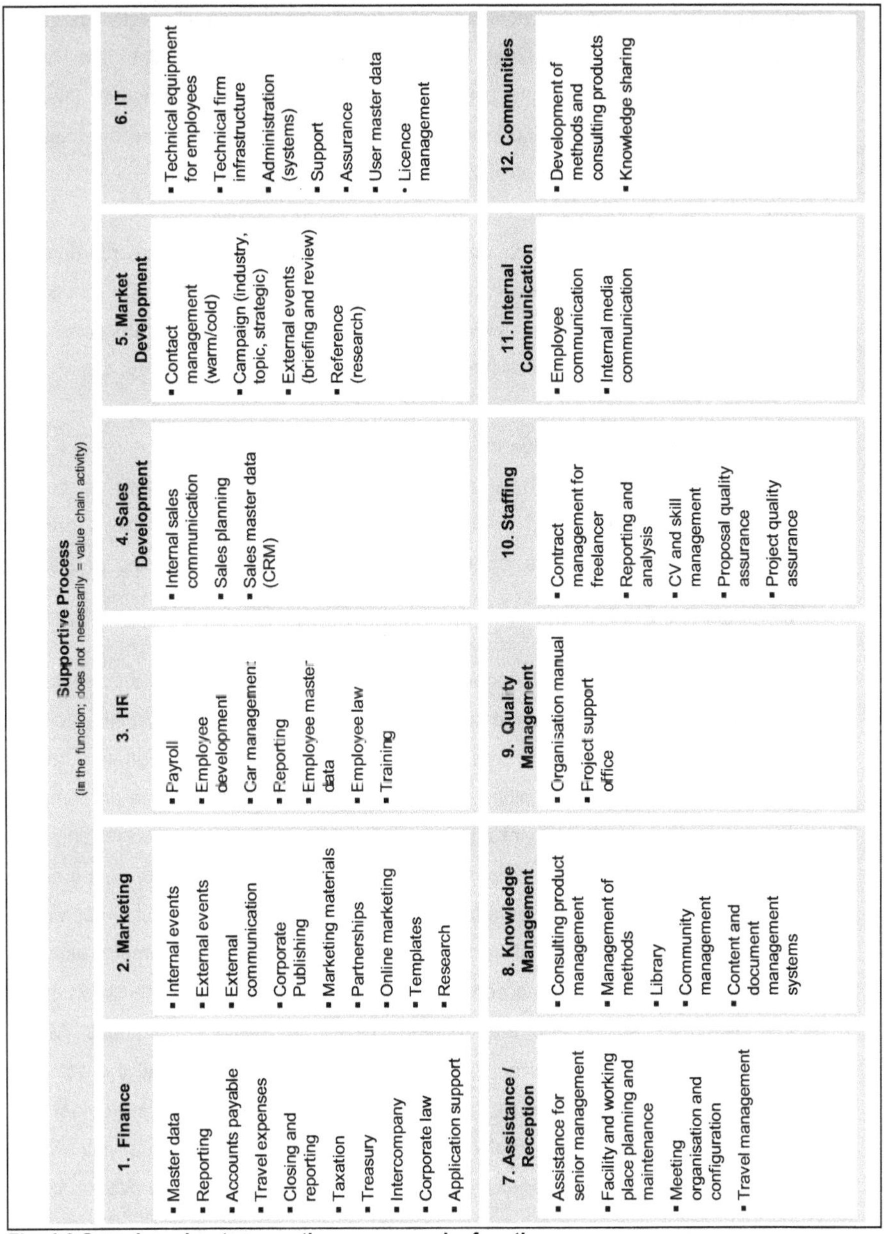

Fig. 4.6 Overview about supportive processes by functions

Routine activities are the executions of the strategy or administrative activities based on internal or external compliance. To be effective with these activities, it is always important that the decision rights are clarified and information flow ensured (Neilson et al. 2008). Administration also includes the coordination of the whole organisation and assurance of fulfilment of all single processes.

Action research: The hypothetical definition is based on secondary research (internal process documentation of the company, general literature relating to the functions). The supportive processes are provided by delivery and corporate functions. The overview of supportive processes by function is summarized in figure **Fig. 4.6**.

4.2.4 Development of the value chain

Within the value chain analysis, all activities of the company need to be re-engineered and dedicated to primary and secondary activities. Porter's primary activities are inbound logistics, operation, outbound logistics, marketing and sales, and after-sales services (Ireland et al. 2009, Mowen and Hansen 2011).

Inbound logistics in a service company are mainly the immaterial factors like people's work (own employees), subcontracted work (freelancer), knowledge, rights etc.; the material factors like computers, cars, office material, literature; and monetary factors like cash and financing possibilities. People's work is the cost intensive portion. The provision and supply of sufficient capacity is the core business of a consulting firm. The recruitment of new employees is based on sales plans, rather than on the actual sales. Capacity building to be able to deliver directly on coming projects is common. Therefore the HR activities of recruiting and employment are primary activities (Dreyer 2003). Operations in a service company are mainly the combination of the factors described above and the maintenance of the delivery readiness (Meyer 1991). Outbound logistics are considered, in a consulting firm, as all the activities needed to provide the service to the customer. Contact between the provider and customer is necessary. This involves a physical, personal, electronically or written contact to the customer. Storage of the service is usually not possible (Meyer 1991). Marketing and sales is responsible for customer relationship management and relationship management of important partnerships. This also involves brand-building activities and boosting a company's image. Both factors are responsible for long term reputation (Meyer 1991). Within the service activities, a company needs to stay in contact with the customer after the project is done, in order to maintain customer satisfaction. Those activities involve after-project support or change requests. Porter's secondary activities are firm infrastructure, human resource management, technology development and procurement (Ireland et al. 2009, Mowen and Hansen 2011). Firms' infrastructures involve company management, finance/controlling and IT. Human resource management includes training, payroll, maintenance and development. IT involves the entire technology infrastructure, which supports all other primary and supportive functions. Procurement is responsible for all materials relating to the company like know how, transportation and communication (Meyer 1991).

In setting up the value chain for the research company, the researcher found it useful to adapt the previously-developed consulting process into the primary activities of the value chain. Those activities are identify and development, sell and entry, planning and staffing, delivery, billing, and termination. The activities relating to "identify and development" and "sell and entry" are denoted as marketing and sales in the value chain. The activities relating to "planning and staffing" are denoted as staffing and recruiting in the value chain. The activities relating to "delivery" are denoted as knowledge management and delivery in the value chain. The activities relating to billing are denoted as billing, and the activities relating to termination as termination in the value chain.

The secondary activities in the research firm are, in the firm infrastructure, provided by IT and facility management, or by human resource management for functions like personnel training, development and maintenance. The other secondary activities are provided by financial management, which includes accounting and controlling, quality management and business support.

Technology development, as part of the traditional value chain, happens partly within the primary activity of knowledge management. Usually, knowledge will be employed within the project, and not as a separate function. One exception appears in communities within the company that develop products and sales kits outside the project work. Such work is rather seen as part of knowledge management, sales, marketing or business support activities. Therefore, the secondary activity technology development was deliberately omitted. Procurement as a further traditional secondary activity was also deliberately omitted, as those activities are part of recruiting and staffing as regards "work" procurement, or part of firm infrastructure as regards offices and IT material procurement. The derivation of the new value chain based on the traditional value chain is shown in figure Fig. 4.7.

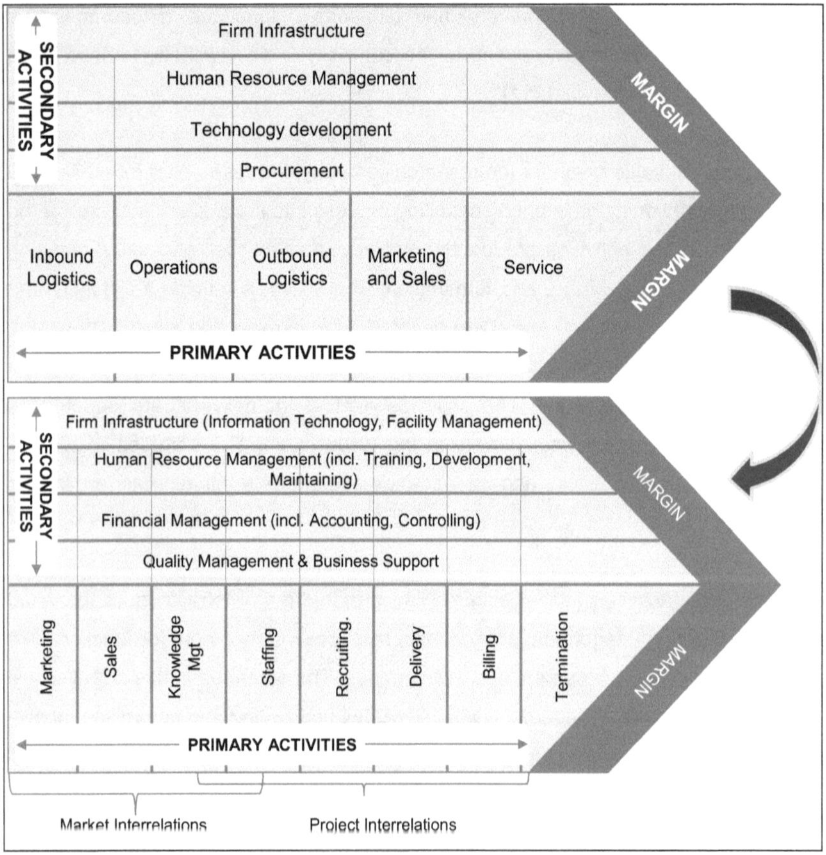

Fig. 4.7 Derivation of traditional VC to a VC of a consulting firm

The assignment of sub processes will take place in the next section, with the help of single process maps, concept for which is also described in the next section.

4.3 Verification phases

4.3.1 Verification hypothetical definition

In this phase, the verification of the hypothetical definition of the main and supporting activities, which were the basis for the development of the value chain, takes place. The verification occurs in interviews with each individual department supervisor. Those supervisors should know exactly which processes within their area are parts of the main process and which support those.

All heads of departments received a short briefing package for their own preparation before the interview meeting. This package contains the objective of the interview, information about the board's support for the project, a brief description of the terminology and handling of the process map system and information about the use of the results in this work. Furthermore, already-prepared process maps are given to the heads of the departments based on the hypotheses about the functions. Those pre-analysis of the processes and cost drivers leads, according to Horváth and Mayer (1993), to an overview of all processes and a provisional structure of the further analysis.

Within the interview, the researcher describes the objectives of the interviews again and goes through each process map. Approvals and adjustments will be made within the interview and documented in the process maps. Missing processes will be added in new process maps.

4.3.2 Value chain analysis process map

The value chain analysis process map system (VCPM) based on the concept provided by the International Group of Controlling (IGC) and has been adapted for the purposes of this study. The structure of the model helps to explain the processes in an uncomplicated, simple way with supported standards templates (IGC et al. 2011). The researcher developed a standard template used for the interviews and based on the templates of the IGC. The content of the template will be explained later. The VCAPM also addresses questions raised by other process maps like the "basic resource activity map" (BRAM) provided by Armistead and Clark (1993). Usually such maps include questions about where value is generated, where the main resources are being used and the main cost of the activity arise. Within the VCAPM model and the standard template, the researcher sets up a hypothetical definition of process maps for each process and validated it in the interview. According to Rathenow (2011) interviewing employees with the best overview of all processes is the recommend procedure.

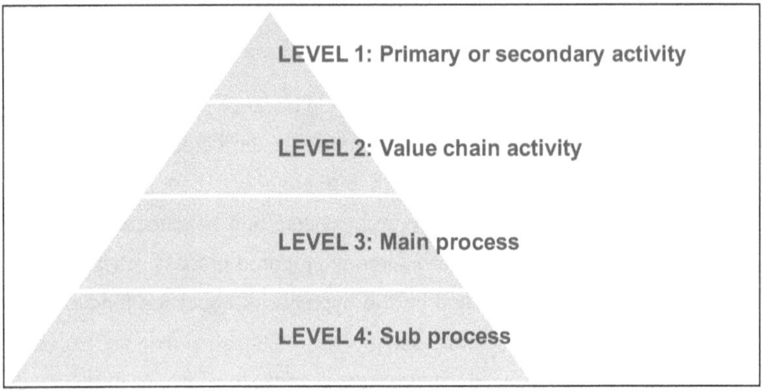

Fig. 4.8 Hierarchy levels of the value chain analysis process map

The VCAPM model has a hierarchical structure (see Fig. 4.8), in which the separation of activities into primary and secondary activities is the first level, and the single value chain activities make up the second level. The difference between both classes and the value chain itself has been already discussed in this study. In general, the second level of the process map hierarchy is the business, or corporate process. The main process of the value chain activity could be the activity itself or a main activity below the value chain activity (process level three). The first case is applicable if the value chain activity is a single process (e.g. billing), while the second case is applicable if the value chain activity is an accumulation (e.g. marketing) of single main processes (brand building, customer relationship management, market development etc.). The structure of the hierarchy is designed to help with understanding to which function and in which context the process is a part of the overall value stream. For the analysis, such a structure is essential.

The middle part of the template describes the process in detail. A process always has a starting point that triggers the process and an end point that closes the process. The length of the period depends on the individual process. Within the value chain analysis process map, this “start of the process” is a separate documentation field, in which those actions that start the process will be filled (process start). The counterpart to this field is the “end of process” field, which identifies those actions that end the process (process end). The fields “input factors / products” and “output factors / products” always describe the inputs and output factor / products that start and end the process. Input and output factors can be any upstream or downstream processes or results that are necessary for conducting the current process, or which assign results to other processes. Between those that start and end, all important and essential sub processes will be recorded. All sub processes together compose the entire main process. The sub processes can take place either one after the other (from top to bottom), parallel (side by side) or independent of each other. Each sub process has always a cost driver.

Cost drivers are those factors that drive the cost of the sub process (Martinson 1994, Mowen and Hansen 2011) in terms of being dependent on variables that raise or reduce the time and effort in the sub process. Such variables, especially in the consulting business, include numbers of projects, number of employees, numbers of travels, consulting hours, travel hours, work hours etc., which are all quantitatively measurable. Cost drivers could be qualitatively or quantitatively measureable factors. As the objective of the study is to set up a cost accounting approach, rather than being based on all measurable factors, the template neglects those qualitative factors, only using them if the overall picture will otherwise be distorted, or if it's essential for the allocation.

The field at the bottom of the template is for the purposes of notifications, further information, validation information and the dedication in the value-adding processes (processes which are part of the primary activities), strategic processes (processes based on company strategy) or routine processes (usually secondary processes). The terminology for this dedication was already given in the previous sections.

The **Fig. 4.9** shows an example of the value chain analysis process map for the main process billing.

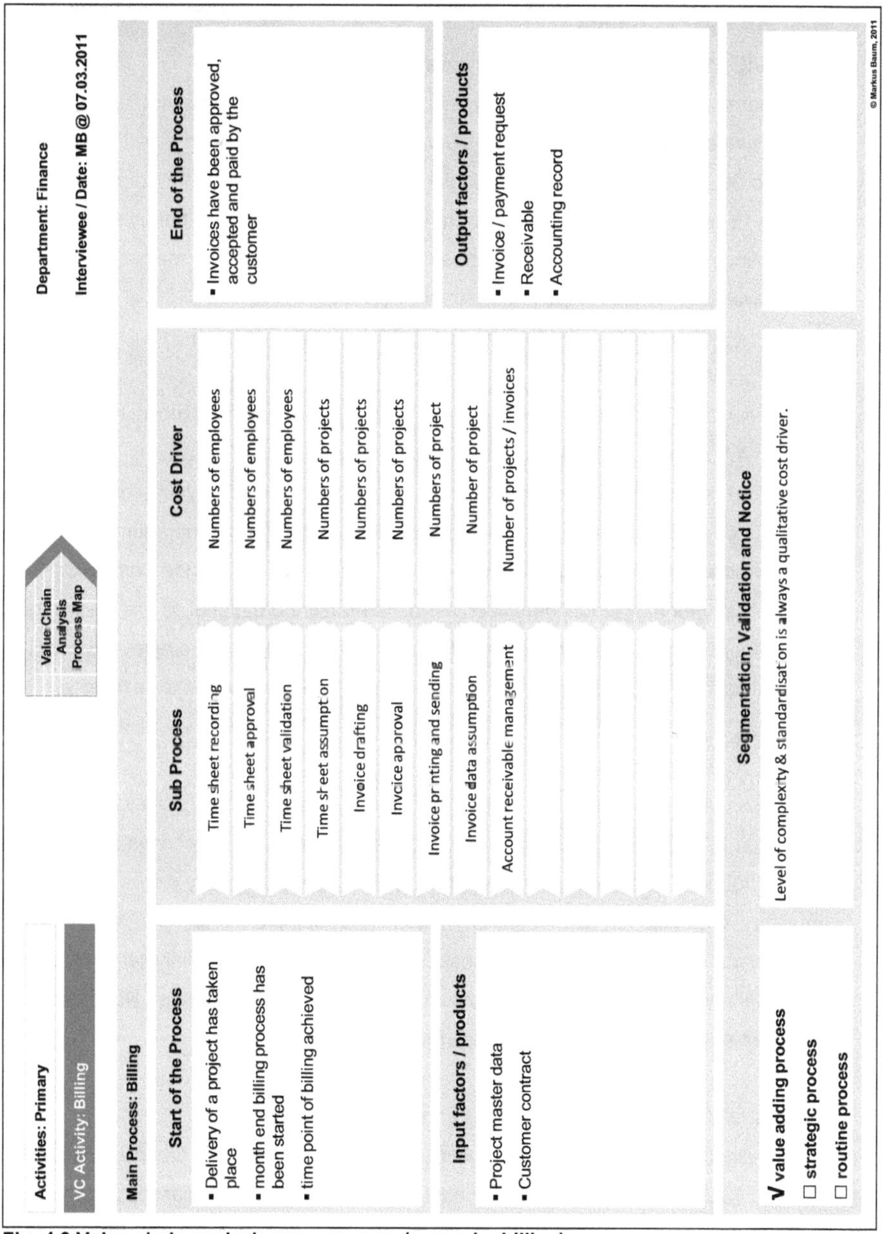

Fig. 4.9 Value chain analysis process map (example: billing)

4.4 Analysis phases

4.4.1 Activity analysis and cost driver analysis

In general, it is necessary to understand that this research cannot amount to a conclusive enumeration of all cost drivers, as each activity has sub activities that also need to be analysed. To adapt the findings of this research for other companies, it is always necessary to respond to company-specific activities and behaviours. Based on the findings of the interviews, in these phases of the study, the main activities and cost driver determined for each department will be reported.

4.4.1.1 Marketing

The main and supportive processes are already listed in the process map (see section 4.2.2 and 4.2.3). Most of the cost drivers within those processes are the time spent (hours of work) on the activity. The activities are usually very different, and their intensity depends on the quality and complexity required for the marketing operation. External costs are also high cost drivers which also depend on the complexity and quality. Only for individual items such as mass marketing material, is the cost drivers the number of the quantity ordered. The number of projects or employees plays a subordinate role. No difference between main and supportive activities exists.

4.4.1.2 Sales

The main and supportive processes are already listed in the process map (see section 4.2.2 and 4.2.3). Most of the cost drivers within those processes are the time spent (hours of work) on the activity. The activities are usually very different, and their intensity dependis on the required quality and complexity for the customer or customers' expectations. External costs are low and include mainly telephone and travel expenses. The number of contacts plays a significant role. No difference between main and supportive activities exists.

4.4.1.3 Knowledge management and quality management

The main and supportive processes are already listed in the process map (see section 4.2.2 and 4.2.3). Most of the cost drivers within those processes are the time spent (hours of work) on the activity. The activities are usually very different, and their intensity depends on the quality and complexity required for the marketing operation.

External costs are low. The number of projects plays a subordinate role. No difference between main and supportive activities exists.

4.4.1.4 Staffing

The main and supportive processes are already listed in the process map (see section 4.2.2 and 4.2.3). Most of the cost drivers within those processes are the available resources and opportunities. The activities are usually standardized and complexity arises with the utilisation. External costs come from the subcontractors whose cost drivers are the bought time. The number of projects plays a subordinate role. No difference between main and supportive activities exists.

4.4.1.5 HR

The main and supportive processes are already listed in the process map (see section 4.2.2 and 4.2.3). HR activities are also discussed at various points in this. Most of the cost drivers within those processes depend on the volume of employees. The activities are usually standardized and complexity arises with the utilisation. External costs are of minor importance. No difference between main and supportive activities exists.

4.4.1.6 Delivery

The delivery has only main activities, which are already listed in the process map (see section 4.2.2 and 4.2.3). Most of the cost drivers within the delivery are the time spent (hours of work) on the activity. The activities are usually very different, and their intensity depends on the quality and complexity required for the project. External costs are low and include mainly telephone and travel expenses. The number of projects or employees plays a subordinate role.

4.4.1.7 Finance

The main and supportive processes are already listed in the process map (see section 4.2.2 and 4.2.3). Most of the cost drivers within those processes depend on the volume of employees, volume of processed invoices (e.g. account payables). External costs are of minor importance. The activities are usually standardised but their intensity depends on the quality and complexity required for the projects.

Differences between main and supportive activities exist. In main activities, the cost drivers are the hours of work, whereby for supportive activities, other measurements drives costs.

4.4.1.8 IT

IT has only supportive processes, which are already listed in the process map (see section 4.2.2 and 4.2.3). Most of the cost drivers within those processes depend on the volume of employees, and volume of systems. External costs are important in terms of purchasing equipment and services. The activities are usually standardised but their intensity depends on the quality and complexity required for the projects.

4.4.1.9 Internal communication

Internal communication has only supportive processes, which are already listed in the process map (see section 4.2.2 and 4.2.3). Most of the cost drivers within those processes are independent of the volume of employees or volume of projects. External costs are of minor importance. The activities are usually standardised but their intensity depends on the quality and complexity required for the content.

4.4.1.10 Business support and reception

The main and supportive processes are already listed in the process map (see section 4.2.2 and 4.2.3). Most of the cost drivers within those processes are the time spent (hours of work) for the activity. The activities are usually very different, and their intensity depends on the required quality and complexity of the expectation. External costs are low and include mainly telephone and travel expenses. The number of employees and prospects plays a significant role. No difference between main and supportive activities exists.

4.5 Interpretation and transfer phases

The analysis of the different activities and operations shows that nearly all units or departments have both main or primary and supportive activities. The most named cost driver of activities that are part of the main processes is the time spent on the work. The volume of those value adding activities depends mainly on the intensity depending on the quality and complexity required for the cases. External spending is of rather minor importance. Supportive activities have both hours of work or a dependent variable magnitude that drives cost. Those activities always have a routine character. If those activities are rather complex, then hours of work is the cost driver. But if those activities are standardized, the dependent variable magnitude drives the cost.

The value chain analysis was executed for the purpose of collecting activities within the company and setting up their value chain. Within the value chain analysis, value adding and routine activities were recorded. Strategic activities were not covered within the value chain analysis model. All activities need to treated separately. The model serves transparency of the company and helps to develop an allocation approach.

The allocation of cost is the focus of this study. Cost allocation based on standard costs, which are developed by the input of historical experience, studies or hypothesis, seems to be the easiest approach as it avoids ongoing documentation. The advantage of this approach is the opportunity for project managers to manage cost by established standards. Standard costs could also align to the current value to start improvement programs (Lanen et al. 2008, pp. 416-449). If a standard cost doesn't fit, variance analysis needs to be done and adjustment is necessary, which in turn is a risk for project managers. Analysis, interpretation, negotiation and communication may lead to a time intensive process. The advantage of cost allocation based on actual cost is that real costs are assigned to the cost object.

In general, the cost allocation of the analyzed activities and operations needs to be based on time spent on all primary activities (value adding activities). To reduce complexity of a cost allocation approach, for routine activities mostly the variable magnitude drivers should be the basis for allocation. However, developing a single allocation approach for each unit and department is recommended, to cover all circumstances. Strategic activities should also be considered in the general allocation approach. Strategic activities were underrepresented in the study. Such activities should not be allocated to projects, but should rather be seen as an investment.

5 Design and development of a costing approach

5.1 Objectives of the new model

The overall objective of a cost accounting model is to inform the management of a consulting firm about the important features and give other stakeholders useful details (needs of decision makers) (Martinson 1994, Lanen et al. 2008). The new model must cover all the costs of the company. Therefore, the costing model must fit to the special issues and situations of a consulting firm. It must cover typical project business and organisational transparency in terms of overhead cost (corporate functions). The entire value chain needs to be covered. Furthermore, the implantation of the costing model must be economically efficient (benefits exceed its costs) and should reduce the complexity of current models.

5.2 Evaluation and selection of the different costing models

Consulting firms are "single product producers", therefore the cost objects are the single projects (internal and external) and are the focus of the cost accounting approach. Projects are the products of a consulting firm; most of them are very individual. Therefore, for consulting firms, the researcher recommends a hybrid-costing model, based on a variable-costing model (for the delivery functions) and an activity-based costing model (for the corporate functions) to cover all issues, such as a business relevant way of working, the allocation of overheads, and the controlling expectations of a management board. The term project should be in the middle of the approach, as it is a common definition in the consulting business. In the following, the new hybrid costing model will be called the service business costing model (SBC model).

Project profitability analysis or project result statements are based on the variable costing model and can be the most important planning and controlling instrument within a consulting firm's cost accounting. It contains all project-relevant monetary incomes and expenses (Stolorz and Fohmann 2005), including calculative costs. In this system, cost objects are the individual internal or external projects. This model will be primarily used for project-related costs (compare section 2.6).

For the allocation of not directly project-related costs (overheads), a system is needed that creates transparency and assists with understanding the cost drivers. Compared to the other costing models, the activity-based costing model is useful for such overhead allocation as it exactly explains the generation of the cost allocation. Activity based costing and management is an important tool for continuous improvement, which should be, in the opinion of the researcher, an overlying objective of corporate functions. In this system, costs for resources will be traced to activities. Activities will be assigned to cost objects (compare section 2.7).

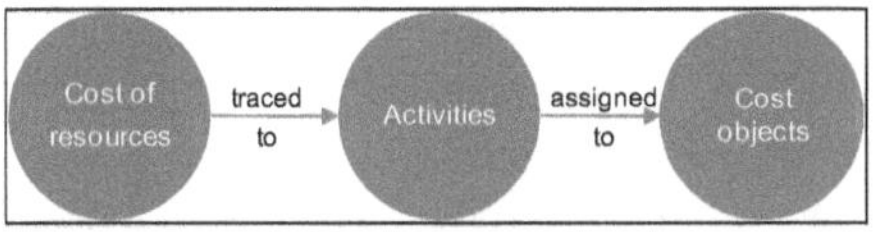

Fig. 5.1 Cost allocation in ABC

The absorption model appears to be ill-fitting to consulting firms, as the model allocates the overhead cost on a proportional basis and can either over or under charge a project, leading to incorrect interpretations (compare section 2.5).

The job order costing model may fit to a consulting firm, but the operational work is very time intensive and does therefore not fit to the objectives (compare section 2.8).

The process costing model does not fit as it's more adaptable to the manufacturing industry (compare section 2.9).

The target costing model does not fit as it is more a basis for the calculation of a project instead of controlling a project (compare section 2.10).

5.3 Design of the cost accounting approach

5.3.1 Service business costing model

The service business costing model (SBC model) is a model developed by the researcher and based on currently available models and close to the ABC model. Within the SBC model, all cost and incomes are assigned to internal and external projects (within an IT system with an own project number).

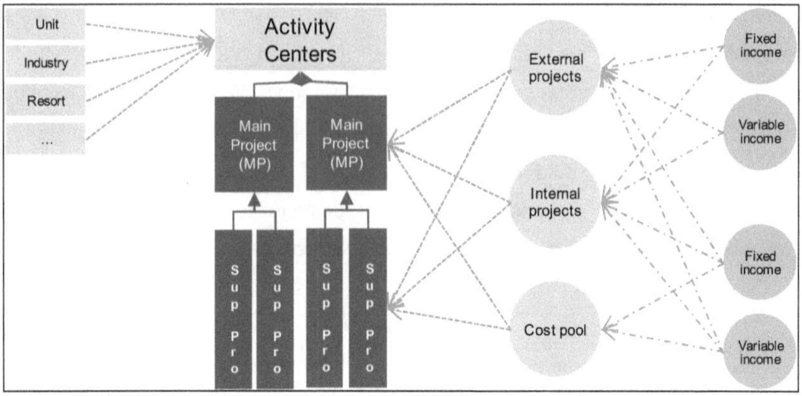

Fig. 5.2 SBC: Sub projects and main projects assigned to activity center

Projects could be either only main projects (MP) or have assigned sub projects (SP) if it is deemed necessary for transparency, operation or allocation purposes. Those projects are the cost objects in the SBC model. Those cost objects could be real projects (e.g. external customer or internal development projects), projects with an exact start and end time point, or cost pools with no start and time point as cost collector (see Fig. 5.2).

All projects are assigned to an activity center (delivery function: DAC or corporate functions CAC), which could be a corporate function, a unit (industry or topic), region, resort, or other profit or cost center. Activity centers are close to or a hybrid of cost centers, revenue centers, profit centers and investment centers (see Fig. 5.3). The proximity to one of the centers depends on the nature of the assigned projects (definition of the centers are stated in Appendix A).

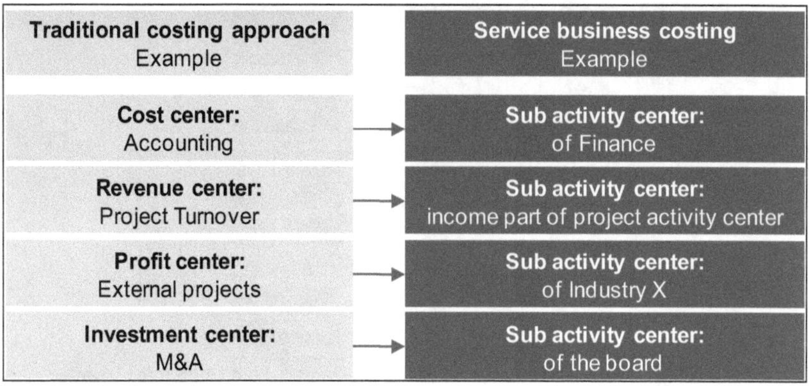

Fig. 5.3 SBC: Terminology traditional costing vs. service business costing

Activity centers have a hierarchal consolidation. Main activity centers (MAC) are dedicated to resort activity center (RAC), RAC are dedicated to delivery activity center (DAC) or corporate activity center (CAC), which are part of the corporate value chain (CVC). MAC as MP could have assigned sub activity centres (SAC), if it is deemed necessary for transparency, operation or allocation purposes. Each activity center has a person responsible for the results and/or allocation of the costs. The objective of the responsible person is to always achieve a high positive result. Activity centers with only costs have the objective of allocating the cost as much as possible to other projects. Their objective is to minimize the negative result. To set up an activity center, each must be detectable by the overall CVC. The hierarchical structure is shown in Fig. 5.4.

The SBC model has a hierarchical structure, as already described. All costs and incomes (fixed cost or income, variable cost or income) will always be assigned to a main or subproject. The results (income minus costs) of the project will be assigned hierarchically from the top, and ends in an activity center. Therefore, the basis for the costing is a project costing approach. The individual parts of the project costing approach are described in the following sections.

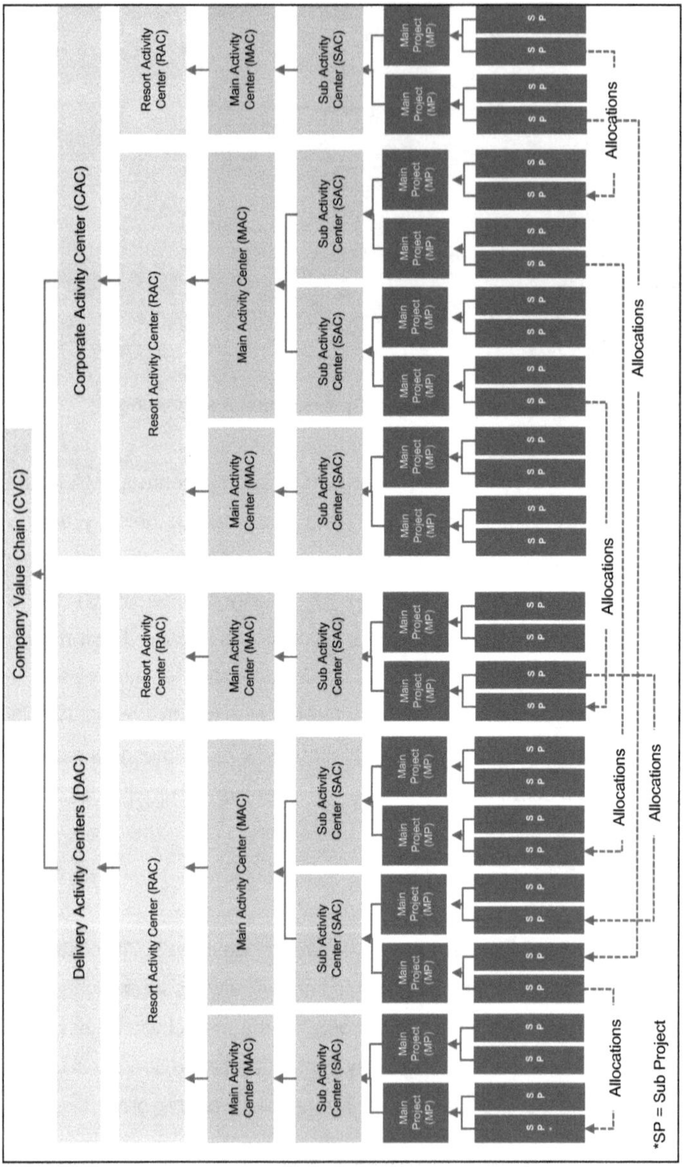

Fig. 5.4 SBC: Hierarchical structure and examples of allocations

Overheads or other costs will also be assigned to a project. Corporate functions usually have projects in which overheads are pooled. The allocation of the cost to other projects is especially important for those overhead costs. The allocations are incomes for such overhead projects and reduce the negative result of the activity center. If an activity center has fixed costs or direct assignable costs itself, the costs will be assigned to a separate (overhead) project, which will be hierarchically assigned to the activity center.

As a resort activity center is usually a department or a person (in a consulting firm for the delivery: partner = resort activity center = partner activity center), it is recommended that at least two main activity centers be set up. One for resort (or partner) overheads and allocations (a separate sub activity center for each), and one for each industry or topic (a separate sub activity center for each customer or topic subtopic). With such a structure, only costs that are not allocated to other projects put stress on the activity center (e.g. non billable hours of consultants remain with the activity center).

In summary, allocation is the focus of the model. Therefore, the activity based costing model fits for this purpose. With the help of the analysis described in section 4.4, the cost driver could be key for cost allocation. An example for the delivery stream of a consulting firm is shown in Fig. 5.5.

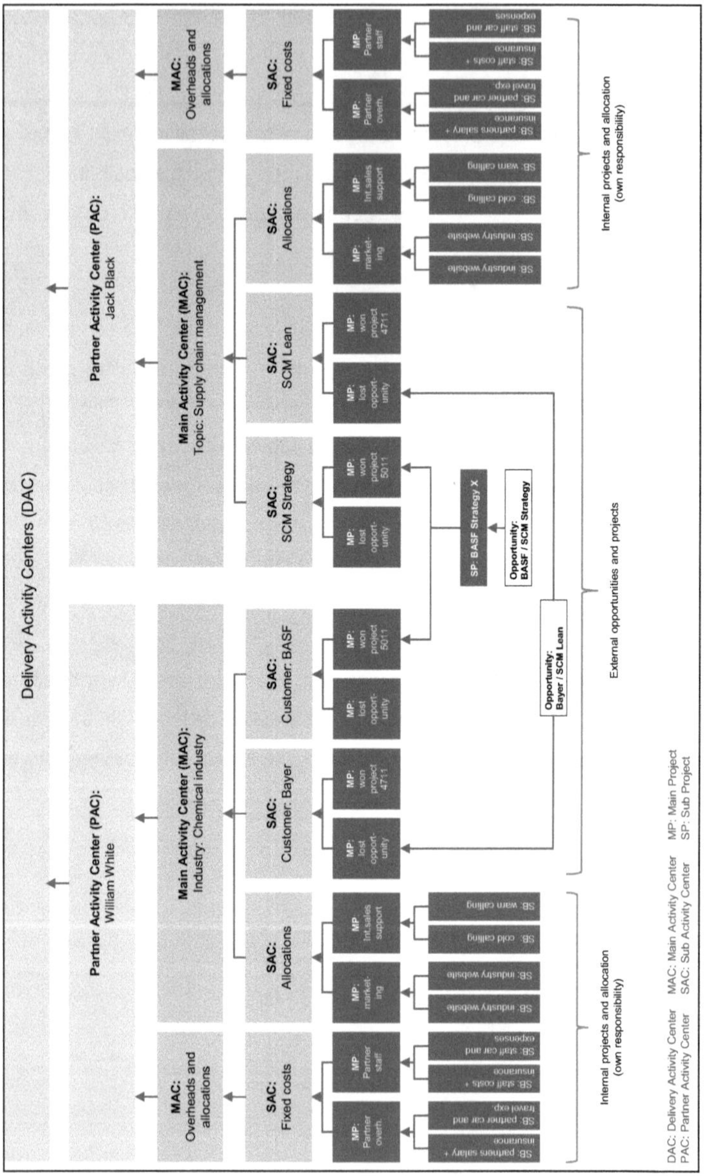

Fig. 5.5 SBC consulting firm example: projects and opportunities

For the allocation of costs, default standard distribution keys could be used if it is ensured that the entire distribution is not above the actual costs. This is only possible if the cost driver lets the costs rise linearly. Otherwise it must be based on the real usage of the activities (e.g. time sheet recording). Complexity within an activity should be considered as a "complexity factor" where the normal allocation key will be multiplied by a complexity factor (e.g. less complexity: allocation key x 1; medium complexity: allocation key x 2; high complexity: allocation key x 3). If complexity is not considered, services may be over or under charged in the opinion of Remer (2005) and lead to incorrect price controlling.

To achieve a precise cost application, the allocation is only possible on MP and SP within the SBC. The hierarchically deeper the allocation happens the more precise the cost application will be, which is the overall objective of the SBC. Allocation on an activity center level is not possible as it would bring the SBC approach closer to the classical costing approaches with their previously discussed shortcomings.

The set up or design of the structure of each activity center is a flexible responsibility of the activity center owner. An example for a consulting firm is given in the next section of this study.

5.3.2 Service business costing model for a consulting firm

As already discussed, a consulting firm has delivery functions and corporate functions. Within the delivery function, a partner (leader) is responsible for a topic, sector or region. Therefore, a partner activity center (PAC) is set up for each partner (or RAC). Within the corporate functions, the responsible persons for the units/departments are the heads of the department. Therefore, the department should be the resource activity center RAC.

Example for delivery function (left case in Fig. 5.5): Partner William White is the leader or the chemical industry. Two customers are assigned to the industry (Bayer + BASF).

1.PAC = Partner White

1.1.MAC = chemical industry

1.1.1. SAC = general allocations to the industry

1.1.1.1. MP: marketing

1.1.1.2. MP: sales

1.1.2. SAC = Customer 1 (Bayer)

1.1.2.1. MP: lost opportunities

1.1.2.2. MP: won project 1

1.1.2.3. MP: won project 2

1.1.3. SAC = Customer 2 (BASF)

1.1.3.1. MP: lost opportunities

1.1.3.2. MP: won project 1

1.1.3.3. MP: won project 2

1.2.MAC = White's own overheads and allocations

1.2.1. SAC = fixed costs

1.2.1.1. MP: personal overheads (e.g. salary)

1.2.1.2. MP: dedicated staff (e.g. assistance)

1.2.2. SAC = variable costs

1.2.2.1. MP: personal overheads (e.g. salary)

1.2.2.2. MP: dedicated staff (e.g. assistance)

In the example above, the industry MAC counts all the results of the customer projects. The overhead and allocation MAC counts all fixed and overhead costs. The Industry MAC needs to finance the overhead MAC.

The allocation of own fixed and overhead costs of the MAC is always an objective for the person responsible for the MAC, as this part can bring negative results to the MAC. For example, the MAC overheads and allocation have their own direct dedicated employees, whose cost needs are allocated to external projects. If the responsible person does not manage to staff all team members on external projects, the non-billed time remains in the SAC and has a negative impact on the overall result of the MAC.

Example for corporate functions: Director John Red is the leader or the HR department (RAC).:

1.RAC = Human Resources
  1.1.MAC = salary
    1.1.1. SAC = management salary
      1.1.1.1. MP: fixed salary
      1.1.1.2. MP: variable salary
    1.1.2. SAC = consultant salary
      1.1.2.1. MP: fixed salary
      1.1.2.2. MP: variable salary
    1.1.3. SAC = corporate function salary
      1.1.3.1. MP: fixed salary
      1.1.3.2. MP: variable salary
  1.2.MAC = personnel development
    1.2.1. SAC = trainings
      1.2.1.1. MP: internal
      1.2.1.2. MP: external
    1.2.2. SAC = events
      1.2.2.1. MP: senior management
      1.2.2.2. MP: all employees
  1.3.MAC = department overheads
    1.3.1. SAC = salary
      1.3.1.1. MP: HR management
      1.3.1.2. MP: HR payroll unit
      1.3.1.3. MP: HR training unit
    1.3.2. SAC = others
      1.3.2.1. MP: expenses
      1.3.2.2. MP: stationery

The allocation of the costs of the HR department is very important. All personnel costs of the company are, in the first step, dedicated to the HR department (MAC: salary) and need to be allocated to all other departments so that no results remain at the MAC HR. If HR recruits people for another MAC, the cost will allocated to the receiver of the new employee.

Using the model could lead to fewer compliance issues or quality management problems as the cost for their management are assigned to the project and reduce the MAC result. In order to counteract and achieve quality and compliance, a project could always be charged with a high standard lump sum for such issues if no allocated costs for such issues are assigned to the project (which suggests that nobody was in charge of the management). Furthermore, another MAC could support those actions and provide positive allocations.

To validate the SBC approach with the reality in the researched consulting firm, the researcher used the entity relationship model from Chen (1976)1. With the help of the model, the researcher designed a logical relationship model for the delivery of the researched consulting firm (see Fig. 5.6) and overlied it on the SBC model (see Fig. 5.7). As no gap between the models exists, the SBC model is valid for and fitting to the researched firm.

---

[1] "The entity-relationship model (or ER model) is a way of graphically representing the logical relationships of entities (or objects) in order to create a database. The ER model was first proposed by Peter Pin-Shan Chen of Massachusetts Institute of Technology (MIT) in the 1970s. In ER modelling, the structure for a database is portrayed as a diagram, called an entity-relationship diagram (or ER diagram), that resembles the graphical breakdown of a sentence into its grammatical parts. Entities are rendered as points, polygons, circles, or ovals. Relationships are portrayed as lines connecting the points, polygons, circles, or ovals. Any ER diagram has an equivalent relational table, and any relational table has an equivalent ER diagram. ER diagramming is an invaluable aid to engineers in the design, optimization, and debugging of database programs.

In a logical sense, entities are the equivalent of grammatical nouns, such as employees, departments, products, or networks. An entity can be defined by means of its properties, called attributes. Relationships are the equivalent of verbs or associations, such as the act of purchasing, the act of repairing, being a member of a group, or being a supervisor of a department. A relationship can be defined according to the number of entities associated with it, known as the degree." (Tech Target 2011)

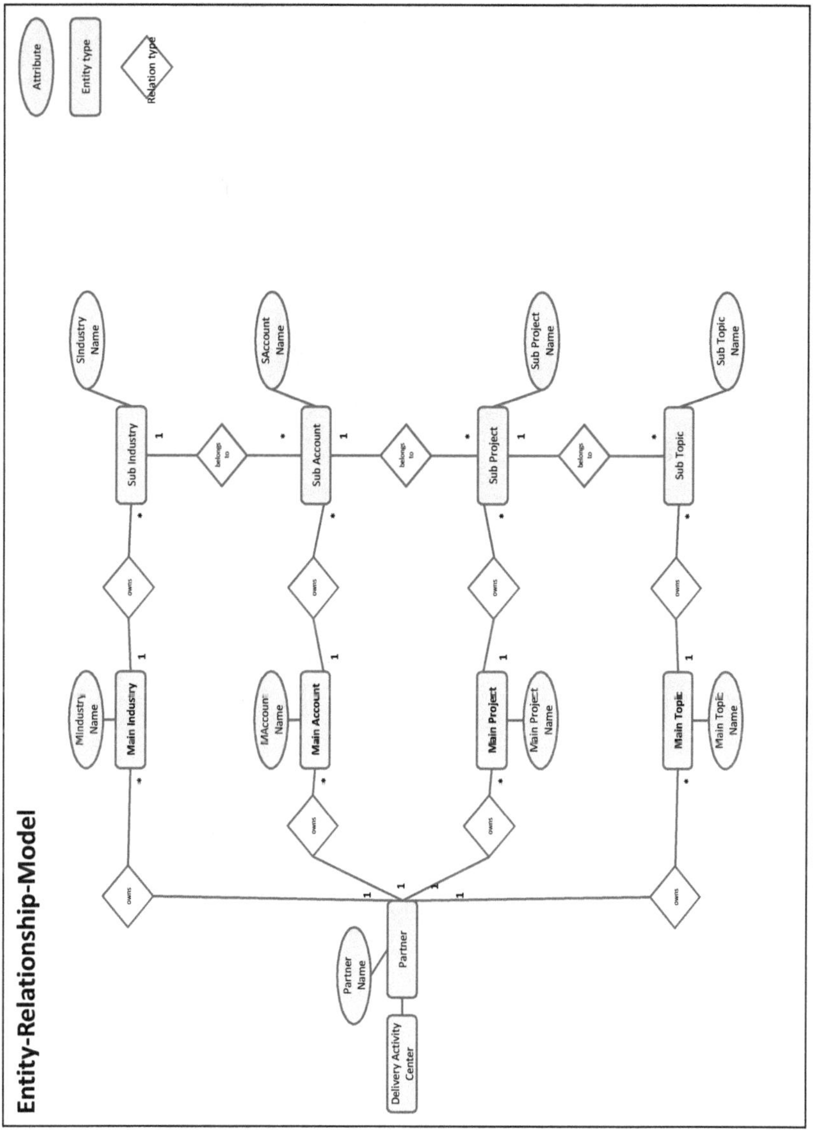

Fig. 5.6 Entity-relationship-model of the researched firm: delivery

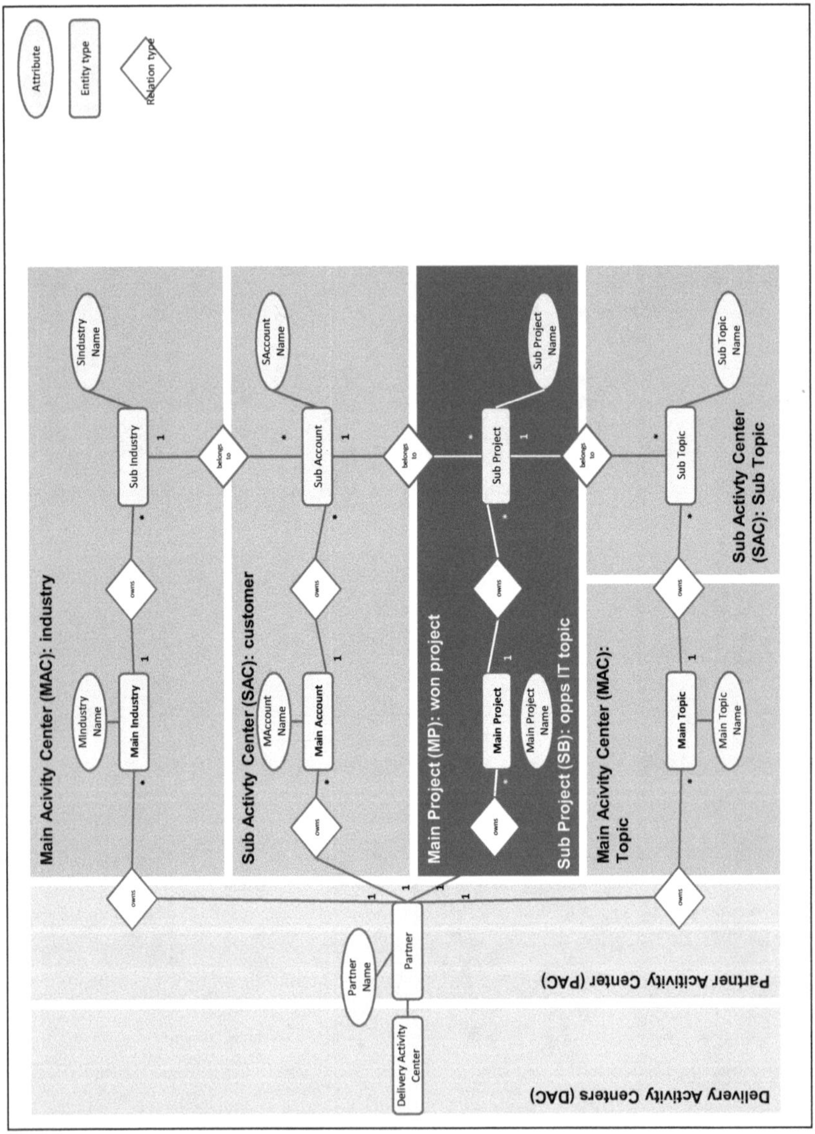

Fig. 5.7 Fit ERM and SBC model of the researched firm: delivery

5.4 Design of the project costing model

As all costs and income are assigned to a project, a project costing model is necessary. The project costing model provides the framework and rules for how cost and incomes will be assigned. The net project result is the sum of total income, total direct costs and total overhead allocation (see Tab. 5.1). Each element or position within the calculation will be briefly described in the following.

1	+	Turnover of the project
2	-	Provisions and reductions
3	+	Income from internal allocation
4	+/-	Work in progress / not billed service
5		**Total income of the project**
6	+	Personnel direct costs - external resources
7	+	Personnel direct costs - internal resources
8	+	Other material direct costs
9		**Total direct cost of the project**
10	+	Personnel overhead costs allocation - external resources
11	+	Personnel overhead costs allocation - internal resources
12	+	Other material overhead costs allocation
13	+	Financing cost
14	+	Cost reductions from internal allocation
15		**Total overhead cost allocation of the project**
16		**Total cost of the project (9+15)**
17		**Net project result**

Tab. 5.1 Calculation scheme of net project result

5.4.1 Turnover of the project

The turnover of the project is all billed consulting services, travel expenses and others like material, licenses or charges. Fixed price rates or value based amounts are part of the consulting services turnover.

5.4.2 Provisions and reductions

Provisions need to be set up if impending losses are expected. They will be reversed if the impending losses are no longer expected or the loss is entered. Reductions are any discounts or reductions in the turnover.

5.4.3 Income from internal allocations

Internal allocations arise through other internal and external projects through offered and ordered services.

5.4.4 Work in progress / not billed service

Work in progress are services that are already delivered but not billed, or the other way around. These incomes need to be valued in the same manner as they would be billed (market value) to value incomes again at the right cost.

5.4.5 Total income of the project

The total income of the project is the sum of all incomes and reductions in the turnover, and presents the income performance of the project (see Tab. 5.2.).

1	+	Turnover of the project
2	-	Provisions and reductions
3	+	Income from internal allocation
4	+/-	Work in progress / not billed service
5		**Total income of the project**

Tab. 5.2 Calculation scheme of total income

5.4.6 Personnel direct costs – external resources

External project resources are usually freelancers or subcontractors who bill their services on their own invoices to the consulting firms. The expenses are dedicated directly to the project.

5.4.7 Personnel direct costs – internal resources

Personnel direct costs are costs that originate through the use of personnel. Such costs are either directly allocated to the project or proportional. Direct costs are those which are explicitly dedicated to the project. Proportional costs are those which are proportionally dedicated to the project.

5.4.7.1 Direct allocation

1	Project travel expenses
2	Project trainings
3	Project bonus
4	Project recruiting costs
5	Project staffing costs
6	**direct project costs (personnel direct costs)**

Tab. 5.3 Calculation scheme of direct personnel projects costs

Direct projects costs can be assigned directly to the project (see Tab. 5.3).

5.4.7.2 Proportional allocation

7	Salary
8	Not project related bonus
9	Overtime premium
10	Vacation and special salary (e.g. Christmas)
11	Social Insurance
12	Other personnel insurance (e.g. disaster)
13	Other benefits
14	Redundancy payment
15	Company car
16	Provision for Vacation
17	Cost of illness
18	Trainings and Development
19	Not project related recruiting
20	Other not project related personnel costs
21	**Proportional allocated project cost (personnel direct costs)**

Tab. 5.4 Calculation scheme of proportionally allocated costs

A concept of how to allocate the proportional cost to a project is always needed and depends on the overall situation. The full cost in the SBC model is always dedicated to a main activity center. Used personnel for projects need to discharge the cost pool.

For the allocation to a project, a day rate based on the individual cost could be calculated and charged, or an average standard rate for a level could be the basis for the allocation.

The advantage of a MAC-specific rate calculation is that all the individual circumstances of the activity center are taken into account.

5.4.8 Other material direct costs

All material costs directly dedicated to the project, such as project equipment (depreciation and lease), software, maintenance of soft- and hardware, office rent for a project, office equipment for a project.

Total direct costs of the project

The total direct cost of the project is the sum of all direct costs dedicated to the project (see Tab. 5.5).

6	+	Personnel direct costs - external resources
7	+	Personnel direct costs - internal resources
8	+	Other material direct costs
9		**Total direct cost of the project**

Tab. 5.5 Calculation scheme of total direct projects costs

5.4.9 Personnel overhead cost allocation – external resources

Administration of external resources like contract management, on boarding, and training is usually managed by central services. Such costs need to be allocated to all projects.

5.4.10 Personnel overhead cost allocation – internal resources

The personnel cost of the management and administrative services are dedicated as overhead costs and need to be allocated to the project.

5.4.11 Other material overhead cost allocation

All material costs of the management and administrative services are dedicated as overhead costs and need to be allocated to the project.

5.4.12 Financing cost

If payment terms are different from the standard terms, the project needs to be charged for this exception. Also, for unusual pricing concepts like fixed priced projects, a risk charge is recommended. In such projects, other projects need to finance such agreements.

5.4.13 Cost reductions from internal allocation

Sometimes projects need to be supported by others or through subvention by internal budgets through strategic decisions or cost reductions.

5.4.14 Total overhead cost allocation of the project

The total overhead cost of the project is the sum of all overhead costs that need to be proportionally allocated to the project (see Tab. 5.6).

10	+	Personnel overhead costs allocation - external resources
11	+	Personnel overhead costs allocation - internal resources
12	+	Other material overhead costs allocation
13	+	Financing cost
14	+	Cost reductions from internal allocation
15		**Total overhead cost allocation of the project**

Tab. 5.6 Calculation scheme of total overheads cost allocation

5.4.15 Total cost of the project

The sum of the direct cost and the proportionally-allocated overhead cost is the total cost of the project.

5.4.16 Net project result

The sum of the total income and the total cost are the net project result of the project.

6 Conclusion and recommendation

Professional service firms have high overhead costs which are difficult to assign to individual service products (projects). High economic pressure on both the cost and revenue sides (Cooper et al. 1996), and the high power of the customer, makes it necessary to understand exactly which functions and operations within the individual organization are value-added, which may not be, and how cost and income can be dedicated to maximizing profit (Kamakura et al. 2002). In summary, professional service firms need costing approaches that bring transparency to their value chain, which helps them find their own improvements in turn.

The classical costing approaches are ill-fitted to professional service firms, as the allocation of overheads is either treated proportionally or is not considered at all. Such allocation frameworks lead to incorrect decisions and bring no transparency to the value chain (Mowen and Hansen 2011).

The absorption costing model is also ill-fitted to professional service firms because the overheads are allocated proportionally as additional fixed parts of the calculation to single products (services). This is only valid at only one volume and cannot provide information concerning a short-term price floor, especially at low or falling utilization, or with enhancing direct costs (Raiborn and Kinney 2009, Mowen and Hansen 2011).

The variable costing seems to be well-fitted to professional service firms, as it shows the project's real valuable contributions to the organisation, but the overhead costs are completely uncovered in this model. If those costs are higher than all the results of the single projects, the projects could appear profitable, but leave the company making a loss (Remer 2005).

The job order costing model may fit to professional service firms, but the operational work for documentation is very time intensive and the cost of running such a system is not proportional (Lanen et al. 2008). The process costing model does not fit as it's more applicable to the manufacturing industry, rather than to professional service firms (Mowen and Hansen 2011). The target costing model does not fit as it is more a basis for the calculation (Lanen et al. 2008, Mowen and Hansen 2011) of a project, instead of for the controlling of a professional service firm.

Activity-based costing (ABC) is useful for overhead allocation, compared to the other costing models, as it exactly explains the generation of the cost allocation. It's less useful for the external projects part (products) of a service firm, as each project has different frameworks and solutions and the model would need to be set up for each project anew, and therefore makes for a complex and expensive system. Setting up an ABC or ABM program always requires a high level of investment, which needs to be repaid by improvements (ROI) (Mowen and Hansen 2011). Therefore monitoring the cost data accurately is also recommended for maintaining the system.

The service business costing model (SBC model) is a hybrid-costing model and a further development of a variable-costing model for delivery functions and an activity-based costing model for the corporate functions. The model has a hierarchical structure in terms of consolidation of the data. The lowest levels within the SBC model are internal and external projects, to which all cost and incomes are assigned. Such projects are upstream consolidated to activity centres, which always have responsible persons. The aim of each activity center is to gather income and allocate costs to and from other centers as much as possible. This aim leads to the condition that all costs and income are assigned to the activities from which they originated.

To set up an appropriate allocation scheme and to analyse the cost of division, an analysis method is needed which creates transparency in all functions of the company. The value chain analysis method of Porter allows for the systematic evaluation of the process and helps to develop an allocation approach. For the purpose of collecting activities within a company and their value chain, this tool, of course with adjustments, is useful in the formulation of the approach (Armistead and

Clark 1993). The service profit chain framework is more valuable as an analysis tool for analysing soft interrelations, rather than for setting up an allocations scheme. Both the value chain and service profit chain frameworks in the consulting industry appear to be under researched, therefore further research is required.

It is recommended, within the implementation of the SBC approach, to dig deeper in the activity analysis and to develop an activity catalogue. Out of it, a cost allocation approach in terms of a fixed allocation key could be developed. The development of this catalogue should be balanced for cost and benefit. The researcher recommends recording each activity that counts for more than 3% of the full time performed by the employee per week. Within a 40 hour week, that means activities with durations of longer than 72 minutes. Activities not represented in the catalogue are not important for the whole value chain. Checking whether such activities could be done with other, lower cost resources, or if they could be omitted, is recommended. The activities within the catalogue should also cover cost drivers, which should have strong connections with the activity center (how could the activity center control the cost driver?). Further cost drivers should also align to the final service (why is the activity important for the company?). Measuring KPIs from the recorded information over a respective period of time may deliver useful insights for controlling productivity or efficiency.

The SBC model has its limitations in covering quality issues, as it considers only measurable values. Qualitative aspects are always cost drivers and usually not measurable within a cost accounting system. Therefore, a separate approach needs to be developed (further research) to cover risks (e.g. quality acceptance procedures and guarantee controlling).

For the service industry in general, a standard structure in terms of approaches and structure needs to be implemented internationally. That would help to provide more transparency and possibilities for benchmarking. Further research and standardising programmes are necessary.

As this study covers only the research of one company, an application to other organizations may be more relevant for some than for others. As the development of a new costing approach (SBC) in this study was only theoretical, its implementation and operation needs to be validated and evaluated in practice. Further research on the implementation and operation of SBC would be interesting and valuable.

7 References

Books

Aharoni, Y. (1997). *Management consulting in changing roles of state intervention in services in an era of open international markets.* New York: State University of New York Press.

Argyris, C., Putnam, R. and Smith, M. (1985). *Action science: Concepts, methods and skills for research and intervention.* San Francisco: Jossey-Bass.

Bryman, A. and Bell, E. (2007). B*usiness research methods.* (2nd ed.). Oxford: Oxford University Press.

Burtonshaw, S. A. (2010). *Essential tools for management consulting: Tools, models and approaches for clients and consultants.* West Sussex: John Wiley and Sons.

Checkland, P. (1981). *Systems thinking, system practices.* New York: John Wiley and Sons.

Christensen, C. M. and Raynor, M. (2003). *The innovator's solution: Creating and sustaining successful growth.* Boston: Harvard Business School Press.

Cooper, R., Kaplan, R., Maisel, L., Morrissey, E. and Oehm, R. (1992). *Implementing activity-based cost management.* Montvale: Institute of Management Accountants.

Creswell, J. W. (2009). *Research design: Qualitative, quantitative, and mixed methods approaches.* (3rd ed.). Thousand Oaks: SAGE Publications.

Davenport, T. and Prusak, L. (2005). Knowledge management in consulting. In L. Greiner and F. Poulfel *Management Consulting Today and Tomorrow.* New York: Routledge.

De Vaus, D. A. (2001). *Research design in social research.* London: SAGE.

Denscombe, M. (2010). *The good research guide: for small-scale social research.* (4th ed.). Buckingham: Open University Press.

Dreyer, D. (2003). *Bewertung personalintensiver Dienstleistungsunternehmen.*Wiesbaden: Springer Science + Business Media.

Duboff, R. (2005). The marketing and selling of consulting service. In L. Greiner and F. Poulfel *Management Consulting Today and Tomorrow.* New York: Routledge.

Fink, D. (2009). *Strategische Unternehmensberatung.* München: Verlag Vahlen.

Fink, D. and Knoblach, B. (2003). *Die großen Management Consultants: Ihre Geschichte, ihre Konzepte, ihre Strategien.* München: Verlag Vahlen.

Gomm, R. and Woods, P. (1993). *Educational research: In action.* London: Paul Chapman Publishing.

Greiner, L. and Malernee, J. (2005). Managing growth stages in consulting firms. In L. Greiner and F. Poulfel *Management Consulting Today and Tomorrow.* New York: Routledge.

Greiner, L. and Poulfel, F. (2005). *Management Consulting Today and Tomorrow.* New York: Routledge.

Henschel, B. (1992). *Dienstleistungsqualität aus Kundensicht.* Wiesbaden: Deutscher Universitäts-Verlag.

Heskett, J. L. and Sasser, W. E. (2010). The service profit chain: From satisfaction to ownership. In P. Maglio, C. Kieliszewski and J. Spohrer, *Handbook of service science: Research and innovations in the service economy.* Berlin: Springer Science + Business Media.

IGC, Heimel, J., Löhnert, P., Michel, U., Ropers, J., Tretter, H., et al. (2011). *Controlling Prozessmodell.* Freiburg: Haufe-Lexware.

Innes, J. and Mitchell, F. (1990). *Activity based costing.* London: The Chartered Institute of Accounting.

Ireland, R., Hoskisson, R. and Hitt, M. (2009). *The management of strategy – concepts and Cases.* (8th ed.). Mason: South-Western Cengage Learning.

Johnson, G., Scholes, K. and Whittington, R. (2008). *Exploring corporate strategy.* (8th ed.). Harlow: Pearson Education.

Kaplan, R. S. and Cooper, R. (1998). *Cost and effect: Using integrated cost systems to drive profitability and performance.* Boston: Harvard Business School Press.

Kubr, M. (2002). *Management consulting. A guide to the profession.* (4th ed.). Geneva: International Labour Organisation.

Lanen, W. N., Anderson, S. W. and Maher, M. W. (2008). *Fundamentals of cost accounting.* New York: McGraw-Hill/Irwin.

Lock, D. (2007). *Project management.* (9th ed.). Hampshire: Gower Publishing.

Lynch, R. (2003). *Corporate strategy.* (3rd ed.). Essex: Prentice Hall Financial Times.

Macmilan, H. and Tampoe, M. (2000). *Strategic management.* Oxford: Oxford University.

Maister, D. (2001). *Practice what you preach: What managers must do to create a high achievement culture.* New York: The Free Press.

Maister, D. (2003). *Managing the professional service firm.* London: Simon & Schuster.

Martinson, O. B. (1994). *Cost accounting in the service industry.* Montvale: Institute of Management Accountants.

Melcher, H. (1982). *Aufbau eines Controllingsystems für Consulting Unternehmen.* Darmstadt: Toeche-Mittler.

Mowen, M. M. and Hansen, D. R. (2011). *Introduction to cost accounting.* (International edn). Spiceland: Cengage Learning Services.

Newman, I. and Benz, C. R. (1998). *Qualitative-quantitative research methodology: Exploring the interactive continuum.* Carbondale and Edwardsville: Southern Illinois University Press.

Nolan, R. and Bennigson, L. (2005). Information technology consulting. In L. Greiner and F. Poulfel, *Management consulting today and tomorrow.* New York: Routledge.

Pfeffer, J. (1994). *Competitive advantage through people: Unleashing the power of the work force.* Boston: Harvard Business School Press.

Porter, M. E. (1980). Competitive Strategy: techniques for Analyzing Industries and Competitors. *Harvard Business School Press* .

Porter, M. E. (1985). *Competitive advantage: Creating and sustaining superior performance.* New York: The Tree Press.

Poulfelt, F., Greiner, L.and Bhambri, A. (2005). The changing global consulting industry. In L. Greiner and F. Poulfel, *Management consulting today and tomorrow.* New York: Routledge.

Remer, D. (2005). *Einführen der Prozesskostenrechnung.* (2nd ed.). Stuttgart: Schäfer Poeschel Verlag.

Riebel, P. (1985). *Einzelkosten- und Deckungsbeitragsrechnung.* Wiesbaden: Gabler.

Riebel, P. (1990). *Einzelkosten- und Deckungsbeitragsrechnung: Grundlagen einer markt- und entscheidungsorientierten Unternehmensrechnung.* (6. ed.). Wiesbaden: Gabler.

Ringlstetter, M. and Bürger, B. (2003). *Bedeutung netzwerkartiker Strukturen bei der strategischen Entwicklung von Professional Service Firms.* Wiesbaden: Gabler.

Ringlstetter, M., Bürger, B. and Kaiser, S. (2004). *Strategien und Management für Professional Service Firms.* Weinheim: Wiley-VCH Verlag.

Saunders, M., Lewis, P. and Thornhill, A. (2009). *Research methods for business students.* (5th edn.). Essex: Pearson Education.

Scott, M. C. (1998). *The intellect industry. Profiting and learning from professional service firms.* West Sussex: John Wiley and Sons.

Shapero, A. (1985). *Managing professional people. Understanding creative performance.* London: Collier Macmillan.

Shenson, H. L. (1990). *How to select and manage consultants.* San Diego: Lexington Books.

Stone, E. (1978). *Research methods in organizational behaviour.* Illinois: Foresmann and Company.

Yin, R. K. (1984). *Case study research, design and methods.* Beverly Hills: Sage Publications.

Journals, newspapers, magazines

Ambos, T. C. and Schlegelmilch, B. B. (2009). Managing knowledge in international consulting firms. *Journal of Knowledge Management.* Vol. 13, No. 6, pp. 491-508.

Armistead, C. G. and Clark, G. (1993). Resource activity mapping: The value chain in service operations strategy. *The Service Industry Journal.* Vol. 13, No. 4, pp. 221-239.

Babad, Y. M. and Balachandran, B. V. (1993). Cost driver optimization in activity-based costing. *The Accounting Review.* Vol. 68, No. 3, pp. 583-575.

Benbasat, I., Goldstein, D. K. and Mead, M. (1987). The case research strategy in studies of information systems. *MIS Quarterly.* Vol. 11, No. 3, pp. 369-386.

Bloch, B. (1999). How get put the "con" in consulting. *Managerial Auditing Journal.* Vol. 14/3, pp. 115-117.

Cooper, D. J., Hinings, C. R., Greenwood, R. and Brown, J. (1996). Sedimentation and transformation in organizational change. The case of Canadian law firms. *Organization Studies.* No. 4, pp. 623-647.

Dawes, P. L., Dowling, G. R. and Patterson, P. G. (1992). Criteria used to select management consultants. *Industrial Marketing Management.,* Vol. 21, pp. 187-193.

Eden, C. and Huxham, C. (1. 7 1996). Action research for management research. *British Journal of Management.* No. 7, pp. 75-86.

Evans, P. and Bellamy, S. (1995). Performance evaluation in the Australian public sector. *International Journal of Public Sector Management*. Vol. 8, No. 6, pp. 30-38.

Hergert, M. and Morris, D. (1989). Accounting data for value chain analysis. *Strategic Management Journal.* Vol. 10, pp. 175-188.

Heskett, J. L., Jones, T. O., Loveman, G. W., Sasser, W. E. and Schlesinger, L. A. (1994). Putting the service profit chain to work. *Harvard Business Review.* No. 03/04, pp. 164-174.

Horváth, P. (1993). Prozesskostenrechnung-Konzeption und Entwicklung. *Die Betriebswirtschaft. Vol. 53, pp. 609-628.*

Horváth, P. and Mayer, R. (1993). Prozesskostenrechnung: Der Weg zu mehr Kostentransparenz und wirkungsvoller Unternehmensstrategien. *Kostenrechnungspraxis: Sonderheft.* No.4, pp. 15-28.

Kamakura, W. A., Mittal, V., de Rosa, F. and Mazzon, J. A. (2002). Assessing the service-profit chain. *Marketing Science*. Vol. 21, No. 3, pp. 294-317.

Kaplan, R. S. and Anderson, S. R. (2007). The innovation of time-driven activity-based costing. *Cost Management.* Vol. 21, No. 2, pp. 5-15.

Ketchen, D. and Hult, G. (2007). Bridging organization theory and supply chain management: The case of best value supply chain management. *Journal of Operation Management.* No. 25, pp. 573-580.

Kolb, D. A. and Frohman, A. L. (1970). An organisation development approach to consulting. *Sloan Management Review.* Vol. 12, No. 1, pp. 51-65.

Loveman, G. W. (1998). Employee satisfaction, customer loyalty, and financial performance: An empirical examination of the service profit chain in retail banking. *Journal of Service Research.* Vol. 1, No. 1, pp. 18-31.

McKenna, C. D. (1995). The origins of modern management consulting. *Business and Economic History*, Vol. 24, No. 1, pp. 51-58.

McLachlin, R. D. (2000). Service quality in consulting: what is engagement success? *Managing Service Quality.* Vol. 10, No. 4, pp. 239-247.

Meyer, A. (1991). Dienstleistungsmarketing. *Die Betriebswirtschaft,* Vol. 51, No. II, pp. 195-209.

Miller, J. G. and Vollmann, T. E. (1985). The hidden factory. *Harvard Business Review*, No. 09/10, pp. 142-15.

Munchus, G. (1989). On the seeking of a definition of management consulting. *Managerial Auditing Journal.* Vol. 4, No. 1, pp. 21-25.

Neilson, G. L., Karla, L. M. and Powers, E. (2008). The secrets to successful strategy Execution. *Harvard Business Review.* No. 6, pp. 61-70.

Normann, R. and Ramirez, R. (1993). From value chain to value constellation: Designing interactive strategy. *Harvard Business Review.* No. 07/08, pp. 65-77.

Patterson, P. G. (1995). Choice criteria in final selection of management consultancy service. *Journal of Professional Services Marketing.* Vol. 11, No. 2, pp. 177-187.

Porter, M. E. (1996). What is strategy? *Harvard Business Review.* No. 11/12, pp. 61-78.

Porter, M. E. (2001). Strategy and the internet. *Harvard Business Review.* No. 3, pp. 63-78.

Porter, M. E. (2008). The five competitive forces that shape strategy. *Harvard Business Review.* No. 1, pp. 78-93.

Raffish, N. and Turney, P. B. (1991). Glossary of activity-based management. *Journal of Cost Management.* Vol. 5, No.3, pp. 53-63.

Rathnow, P. (2001). Effektive Unternehmenswwertsteigerung durch Activity-Based-Management. *Controller Magazin.* No.3/4, pp. 48-52.

Shields, M. (1995). An empirical analysis of fims' implementation experiences with activity-based costing. *Journal of Management Accounting Research.* Vol. 7, pp. 148-166.

Shields, M. and Young, S. M. (1989). A behavioural model for implementing cost management systems. *Journal of Cost Management.* Winter, pp. 17-27.

Internet article and sources

EU. (2010). *Der EU Binnenmarkt.* Available at http://ec.europa.eu/internal_market/ top_layer/index_19_de.htm. [Accessed 08. January 2011].

FEACO. (2009). *Survey of the European management consultancy 2008/2009.* Available at http://www.mca.org.hk/FEACO%20Survey%202009%20final.pdf. [Accessed 03. April 2011].

FEACO. (2010). *FEACO Market information 2009.* Available at http://www.feaco.org /en/index-action-marketInformation.html. [Accessed 21. February 2011].

Glückler, J. (2005). *Management consulting: structure and growth of a knowledge intensive business service market in Europe.* Available at http://publikationen.ub.uni-frankfurt.de/volltexte/2005/602/. [Accessed 08. February 2011].

ICMCI. (2002). *The common body of knowledge.* Available at http://static.icmci.org/ download/?id=1845879. [Accessed 22. February 2011].

ICMCI. (2011). *IMC: about the institute.* Available at http://www.imcsa.org.za/Home/ AbouttheInstitute/tabid/231/Default.aspx. [Accessed 29. March 2011].

Kaplinsky, R. and Morris, M. (2002). *Institute of Development Studies: A handbook for value chain research.* Available at http://www.inti.gov.ar/cadenasdevalor/ manualparainvestigacion.pdf. [Accessed 26. February 2011].

Tech Target. (2011). *Definition entity-relationship model.* Available at http://searchsqlserver.techtarget.com/definition/entity-relationship-model. [Accessed 04. April 2011].

Trochim, W. M. (2006). *Ethics in research.* Available at http://www.socialresearchmethods.net/kb/ethics.php. [Accessed 21. March 2011].

University of Surrey. (2001). Code on good research practice. Available at http://www.surrey.ac.uk/fahs/staffandstudents/ethicalprocedures/documents/code_on_good_research_practice.htm [Accessed 02. April 2011].

Studies, not public sources

BDU. (2010). *Facts & Figures zum Beratungsmarkt 2009/2010.* Study. Bonn: BDU.

Lünendonk. (2010). *Lünendonk-Studie 2010: Führende Managementberatungs-Unternehmen in Deutschland.* Study. Kaufbeuren: Lünendonk.

APPENDIX A

Cost accounting terminology used in the study

Actual costs	Costs that are "determined by actual direct material and labour costs plus overhead applied using an actual overhead rate and an actual allocation base" (Lanen et al. 2008, p. 222).
Batch-level costs	Batch-level costs "...are caused by a group of things being made, handled, or processed at a single time..."; types of costs are purchase orders, setup, inspection, movement; and are incurred once for each batch produced (Raiborn and Kinney 2009, p. 107).
Cost	"Cost reflects the monetary measure of resources expended to attend an object such as making a good or delivering a service." (Raiborn and Kinney 2009, p. 107). Simplified, cost is a sacrifice of resources (cash or cash equivalent) (Lanen et al. 2008) that are expected to bring a current or future benefit to the company (Mowen and Hansen 2011). Expenses, in contrast to the term cost, are costs that are charged against revenue in an accounting period (Mowen and Hansen 2011).
Cost allocation	Cost allocation is the "process of assigning indirect costs to products, services, people, business unit" and other cost objects (Lanen et al. 2008, p. 42). Specific allocation rules support the process.
Cost center	Cost center is a subunit of an organisation, which is only responsible for costs. The performance will be measured by

	the volume of costs and the keeping of the budget and has partly no direct relation to the output of the company.
Cost center accounting	Cost center accounting spreads the overhead costs between the sites of emergence. Cost center accounting is regularly used for monitoring cost centers and for the indirect allocation of operational performance to cost objects. Cost centers are also called cost pools which are the collection of cost (Lanen et al. 2008).
Cost driver	A "cost driver" is an activity or predictor (activity measurer) which, due to a cause-and-effect relationship, drives costs (Martinson 1994, Lanen et al. 2008, Mowen and Hansen 2011).
Cost element accounting groups	Cost element accounting groups the costs into direct costs (single costs) and indirect costs (overall costs).
Cost object	The "cost object" is one of the most important terms as it refers to each object (product, service, project, etc.), used as a collector or accumulator of costs, usually as defined by the management. Cost objects are the end to which a cost is assigned (Lanen et al. 2008, Mowen and Hansen 2011). In consulting firms, most cost objects (e.g. service costs) are usually internal and external projects. Those projects are different in terms of quality, time, place and value (Reckenfelderbäumer 1995). According to the relationship to cost objectives, the cost can be categorised into the following:

Association with cost object:

1. Direct costs: any cost that can be directly related to a cost object
2. Indirect cost: any cost that cannot be directly related to cost object

Components of product cost:

1. Direct material cost: any cost that can be directly identified as part of a product
2. Direct labour: any effort of individuals that can be directly identified as part of a product
3. Production overhead: any cost that can be indirectly related to the product

Reaction to changes in activity:

1. Variable cost: cost that fluctuates and varies in direct proportion with a change in volume
2. Fixed cost: cost that is unchanged with volume changes and remains constant in total
3. Mixed cost: cost that has variable cost parts and fixed-cost parts
4. Step cost: cost that increases at certain activity levels

Classification of the financial statements:

1. Unexpired: cost that is reported in the balance sheet
2. Expired: cost that is reported in the income statement
3. Product: cost that is prime or conversion part of a product
4. Period: cost that is expensed in a specific period for financial reporting

Classification of organisational costs:

1. Upstream cost: cost that arise before the production (e.g. research, development)
2. Downstream costs: cost that arise after the production (e.g. marketing, sales)

	(Raiborn and Kinney 2009, Lanen et al. 2008, Mowen and Hansen 2011).
Cost object accounting	Cost object accounting has the purpose of allocating the cost from the cost element accounting to the cost objects. In the service industry, it is sometimes difficult to find individual cost objects, as it is often the case that no direct relationship to the service product exists. Because of the individuality of the performance, it is difficult to set up a standardized allocation or an allocation on average. In consulting firms, the individual projects (internal and external) are the cost objects (Reckenfelderbäumer 1995).
Cost pool	A "cost pool" or activity center is an accumulator of costs on different levels (unit-level, batch-level, product/process-level, organizational level) (Raiborn and Kinney 2009).
Functions of cost accounting	**Documentation:** Recording the actual costs incurred in one period (one set price and quantity required), transferring cost to cost objects. Combination of formal and informal recordkeeping (Raiborn and Kinney 2009, Mowen and Hansen 2011). **Information, planning and control:** Orientation, foundation and control of decisions, cost information and tasks (Bertsch 1991). The information is current or forecasted, quantitative or qualitative, and monetary or non-monetary (Raiborn and Kinney 2009, Mowen and Hansen 2011). **Conflict resolution and decision making:** Argumentation and transparency, information to resolve conflict (Mowen

	and Hansen, 2011).
Investment center	Investment center is a subunit of an organisation which is responsible for profits and investments in assets (Lanen et al. 2008).
Normal costs	Costs that are "determined by actual direct material and labour costs plus overhead applied using a predetermined rate and an actual allocation base" (Lanen et al. 2008, p. 222).
Organizational-level costs	Organizational-level costs "...are incurred for the sole purposes of supporting facility operations"; types of costs are building depreciation, division managers' salary, organizational advertising; support for the overall production or service process (Raiborn and Kinney 2009, Mowen and Hansen 2011).
Product-level/ process-level costs	Product-level/process-level costs are "...caused by the development, production, or acquisition of different items..."; (Raiborn and Kinney 2009, 108) types of costs are engineering change orders, equipment maintenance, product development; support for a product type or process (Mowen and Hansen 2011).
Profit center	Profit center is a subunit of an organisation which is responsible for revenue and cost together (=profit).
Revenue center	Revenue center is a subunit of an organisation only responsible for revenue. The performance will be measured by the volume of revenue which also may lead to suboptimal behaviour in terms of cost consciousness.

Standard (plan) costs	Costs that are "determined by standard (budgeted) direct material and labour costs plus overhead applied using a predetermined overhead rate and an standard (budgeted) allocation base" (Lanen et al. 2008, p. 222).
Unit-level costs	"Unit-level costs are caused by the production or acquisition of a single unit of product or the delivery of a single unit of service"; (Raiborn and Kinney 2009, p. 107) types of costs are direct material, direct labour and some machine costs, if traceable; and are incurred once for each unit produced (Mowen and Hansen 2011).

APPENDIX B

Briefing package interviews

All heads of departments received a short briefing package (see following slides) for their own preparation before the interview meeting. This package contains the objective of the interview, information about the board's support for the project, a brief description of the terminology and handling of the process map system and information about the use of the results in this work. Furthermore, already-prepared process maps (see examples below) are given to the heads of the departments based on the hypotheses about the functions.

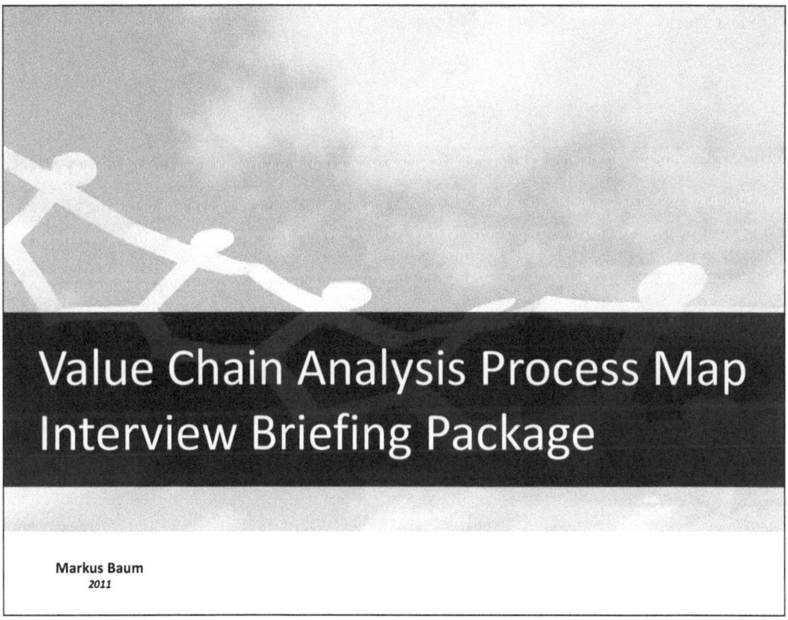

Many thanks for your participation!

Welcome to the briefing package

Dear colleague,
I am currently evaluating, on behalf of the board, the introduction of a cost accounting approach. My research focus is the selection of a suitable method and structural construction.
To make this evaluation successful, I need your help. As a team leader responsible for important processes, you are, of course, the best contact for this matter.
In an interview, I would like to discuss and verify the processes and approach I have already set up hypothetically.
This intention of this document is to inform you before the interview about the intention, methods used and agenda.
Thank you for your cooperation in advance and best regards
Markus Baum

Markus Baum
Group Finance Director

Content

Briefing package

1 Objectives and methods

2 Background and terminology

3 Agenda and interview content

4 List of processes (value chain oriented)

5a Value chain anlaysis process map (example hypothesis) – Primary Activities

5b Value chain anlaysis process map (example hypothesis) – Secondary Activities

Objectives and methods

Project and Interview

Project objectives

- Evaluation of fitting cost accounting approaches
- Development and adoption of a cost accounting approach
- Development of allocation keys
- Preparation for an implementation project

Interview objectives

- Discussion of the important main and supportive processes of the department/unit
- Discussion and verification of hypothesis concerning main and supportive processes maps
- Introduction to the cost driver approach and discussion
- Discussion of value adding, strategic and routine process approaches

Please note: the whole project has a research character. It is therefore not necessary to go to into depth.

Methods

- Interview
- Setup and examination of the overall process map for each function (department/unit)
- Value chain analysis process map

Terminology

Value chain, processes and activities

Value chain analysis

The value chain analysis breaks companies' value chains down into individual activities. The method allows the firm to understand which parts of its operations create value and which do not (Ketchen und Hult 2007). The aim is to cut the entire complicated supply chain of a company into smaller units. The value chain contains primary and secondary activities

Primary and secondary activities

Primary activities are those involved in a product's physical creation, sales and distribution, and after-sales service. Support activities provide the assistance necessary for primary activities (Ireland, Hoskisson und Hitt 2009, 71-89).

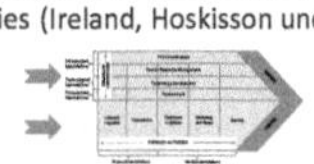

Main and supportive processes

Main processes are all processes that are part of the primary activities in the value chain. Supportive processes are those activities that support the main process. They are not part of the primary activities. This doesn't mean that those activities are not important or that these activities are worthless, those activities are rather routine, or strategic activities, instead of value adding by definition.

Value adding, routine, strategic activities

Value-adding activities can, by definition, only be primary activities. Secondary activities are not value adding as a customer receives no direct value from them. Strategic activities are those activities and operations that create (development) or are aligned with (strategy execution) a company's strategy. Routine activities are the executions of the strategy, or administrative activities based on internal or external compliance.

Terminology

Cost accounting and value chain process map

Cost accounting

Cost accounting is part of internal management accounting. Costs and incomes will be assigned to different cost objects, which are again assigned to responsible persons/units. In general, cost accounting has the function of documentation, information, planning, control and conflict resolution.

Cost objects

Cost objects are collectors or accumulators of costs and income. They are usually defined by the management of a function. For a consulting firm, the cost objects are usually internal and external projects.

Cost driver

Cost drivers are those factors which drive the cost of the sub process (Mowen und Hansen 2011, 534) in terms of dependent variables which raise or reduce the time and effort of the sub process. Such variables, especially in the consulting business, include numbers of projects, number of employees, amount of travel, consulting hours, travel hours, work hours etc. that are all quantitatively measurable.

Value chain analysis process map

The value chain analysis process map is a standard template that helps to explain the processes in an uncomplicated simple way. It includes information about actions which start/end the process, and which inputs/outputs are generated. Within the template, a main process is divided into sub processes with their own individual cost drivers.

Background

Primary activities of a consulting firm

I. Acquisition Phase		II. Execution Phase		III. Finalizing / Post-Project Phase	
1. Identify and Development	**2. Sell and Entry**	**3. Planning and Staffing**	**4. Delivery**	**5. Billing**	**5. Termination**
• Industry and Customer research / assessment • Project enhancement • Warm and cold calling, key-account management • Market development • Branding • Customer relationship management	• First contacts with client • Preliminary problem diagnosis • Assignment planning • Assignment (or presentation) of proposals to client • Consulting contract • RFP • Proposal quality assurance	• Evaluating existing solutions or methods • Proposal of solutions to client • Planning for implementation • Team staffing • Training • Recruiting • Subcontracting	• Fact analysis and synthesis • Detailed problem examination • Adapting or developing solutions • Implementation (or assisting with) • Training / knowledge transfer • Project mgt./ controlling/ change management • Change requests • Time and expenses recording	• Contract management • Master data management • Invoicing • Accounts receivable management	• Evaluation • Final report / documentation • Customer acceptance report • Settling commitments • Plans for follow-up • Knowledge transfer to the own firm (knowledge management) • References

Background

From a classical value chain to the value chain of a consulting firm

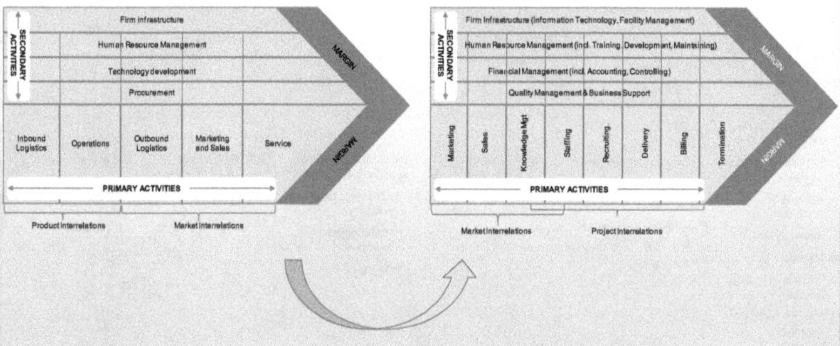

Agenda and interview

Preparation for the meeting, interview content, after meeting actions

Before the meeting	The researcher has developed a hypothetical map of all main and supportive process assigned to the different functions. Derived from this hypothetical value chain analysis, process maps for all important main process and samples of supportive processes are developed. The maps are part of this package.
Introduction	At the beginning of the meeting, a short introduction to the project, the methods, terminology and objective of the interview will be given. Most of the information is already provided within this package.
Interview	Within the interview, the hypothetical definitions of the maps will be discussed, verified and supplemented. In addition, general information about the responsibilities, cost drivers of the functions and input for the development of a cost accounting approach will be collected. The maps are part of this package.
After the meeting	After the meeting, the researcher analyses the results of the meeting and uses the data for a value chain analysis and the development of a cost accounting approach .

Main Process
(in the function; does not necessarily = value chain activity)

Delivery

- Project enhancement
- Key account mgt.
- First contacts with client
- Preliminary problem diagnosis
- Assignment planning
- Assignment of proposals to client
- Consulting contract
- RFP
- Evaluating existing solutions
- Proposal of solutions to client
- Planning for implementation
- Team staffing
- Training
- Fact analysis and synthesis
- Detailed problem examination
- Adapting or developing solutions
- Assisting with/and implementation
- Training / knowledge transfer to the customer
- Project management / controlling / change management
- Change requests
- Time and expenses recording
- Evaluation
- Final report / documentation
- Customer acceptance report
- Settling commitments
- Plans for follow-up
- Withdrawal
- Knowledge transfer to own firm
- References

1. Finance

- Time and expenses recording
- Project controlling
- Contract management
- Project master data management
- Invoicing
- Accounts receivable management

2. Marketing

- Branding
- CRM
- References
- Direct Marketing

3. HR

- Recruiting
- Training (administrative)

4.&5. Market & Sales Development

- Industry and customer research
- Warm and cold calling
- First contact with clients

7. Assistance / Reception

- Industry and customer research
- Time and expenses recording

8.+9. Knowledge & Quality Management

- Evaluating existing solutions
- Knowledge transfer to own firm
- Training (content)

10. Staffing

- Team staffing
- Subcontracting

12. Communities

- Support for sales and marketing

Supportive Process
(in the function; does not necessarily = value chain activity)

1. Finance

- Master data
- Reporting
- Accounts payable
- Travel expenses
- Closing and reporting
- Taxation
- Treasury
- Intercompany
- Corporate law
- Application support

2. Marketing

- Internal events
- External events
- External communication
- Corporate Publishing
- Marketing materials
- Partnerships
- Online marketing
- Templates
- Research

3. HR

- Payroll
- Employee development
- Car management
- Reporting
- Employee master data
- Employee law
- Training

4. Sales Development

- Internal sales communication
- Sales planning
- Sales master data (CRM)

5. Market Development

- Contact management (warm/cold)
- Campaign (industry, topic, strategic)
- External events (briefing and review)
- Reference (research)

6. IT

- Technical equipment for employees
- Technical firm infrastructure
- Administration (systems)
- Support
- Assurance
- User master data
- Licence management

7. Assistance / Reception

- Assistance for senior management
- Facility and working place planning and maintenance
- Meeting organisation and configuration
- Travel management

8. Knowledge Management

- Consulting product management
- Management of methods
- Library
- Community management
- Content and document management systems

9. Quality Management

- Organisation manual
- Project support office

10. Staffing

- Contract management for freelancer
- Reporting and analysis
- CV and skill management
- Proposal quality assurance
- Project quality assurance

11. Internal Communication

- Employee communication
- Internal media communication

12. Communities

- Development of methods and consulting products
- Knowledge sharing

Activities: *Primary or Secondary*

VC Activity: *out of the value chain*

Handling the template: Introduction

Department: *interviewed department*

Interviewee / Date: *person@dd.mm.yy*

Main Process: *description of the process*

Start of the Process	Sub Process	Cost Driver	End of the Process
Activities and operations which trigger the process	*Between those start and end conditions, all important and essential sub Processes will be recorded. All sub Process together compose the whole main process. The sub processes can take place either one after the other (from top to bottom), parallel (side by side) or independent of each other.*	*Cost drivers are those factors which drive the cost of the sub process (Mowen und Hansen 2011, p. 534) in terms of dependent variables which raise or reduce the time and effort of the sub process. Such variables, especially in the consulting business, include numbers of projects, number of employees, amount of travel, consulting hours, travel hours, work hours etc. which are all quantitatively measurable. Qualitative, not quantitatively measureable factors are also cost drivers but not in focus*	*Activities and operations which close the process*

Input factors / products

Input factor / products which bring the process to the start. Input factors can be any upstream processes or results, which are necessary to reach the current state

Output factors / products

Outputs factors / products can be any downstream processes or results, which come out of the current process or which assign results to other processes

Segmentation, Validation and Notice

√ **value adding process**
☐ **strategic process**
☐ **routine process**

This field can be used for any comments regarding the segmentation and validation

This field can be used for any notice

Activities: Primary

VC Activity: Sales

Value Chain Analysis Process Map

Department: Sales / Assistance
Interviewee / Date: TW@10.03.11
AG@10.03.11
MR@17.03.11
MK@16.03.11

Main Process: Sales cycle

Start of the Process	Sub Process	Cost Driver	End of the Process
▪ Sales activities	Identification	Hours of work/ external spending	▪ Project-won
	Qualification	Hours of work/ external spending	▪ Project-loss
	Conception	Hours of work/ external spending	
	Proposal	Hours of work/ external spending	
	Win or Loss Situation	Hours of work/ external spending	

Input factors / products

▪ Sales strategy
▪ Company strategy

Output factors / products

▪ Project or lost opportunity

Segmentation, Validation and Notice

√ **value adding process**
☐ **strategic process**
☐ **routine process**

Activities: Primary

VC Activity: Staffing

Value Chain Analysis Process Map

Department: Staffing

Interviewee / Date: CR@17.03.11

Main Process: Team Staffing

Start of the Process

- Project or opportunity needs to be staffed

Sub Process	Cost Driver
Request occupation	Number of projects / opportunities
Identification of resources	Number of resources
Check availability of resources	Number of resources
Selection of the team	Number of resources
Information to all stakeholders	Number of projects / opportunities
Reservation of staff	Number of resources
Travel cost optimisation	Number of resources

End of the Process

- Project or opportunity has been staffed

Input factors / products

- Project / opportunity information
- CV
- Information systems

Output factors / products

- Project / opportunity team

Segmentation, Validation and Notice

√ value adding process

☐ strategic process

☐ routine process

Utilisation has impact on cost driver

Content

Briefing package

Activities: Secondary

VC Activity: Financial Management

Value Chain Analysis Process Map

Department: Finance

Interviewee / Date: MB@13.03.11

Main Process: Transfer pricing strategy

Start of the Process

- New strategy needs to be developed

Sub Process	Cost Driver
Approach development	Hours of work/ external spending
Approach implementation	Hours of work/ external spending

End of the Process

- Strategy developed and implemented

Input factors / products

- Finance strategy
- Company strategy
- Law

Output factors / products

- Documentation
- Operating procedures
- Policies

Segmentation, Validation and Notice

☐ value adding process
√ strategic process
☐ routine process

No direct receiver of the work, usually the whole company or entities

Activities: Secondary

VC Activity: Human Resource Mgt.

Value Chain Analysis Process Map

Department: HR

Interviewee / Date: MI@17.03.11

Main Process: Payroll

Start of the Process

- Monthly pay slip needs to be prepared

Sub Process	Cost Driver
Announcement for new employees	Numbers of new employees
Adjustments to existing employees	Numbers of employees
Master data maintenance	Numbers of employees
Data proceeding	Numbers of employees
Payslip results and quality assurance	Numbers of employees
Payslip sending	Numbers of employees
Payment	Numbers of employees

End of the Process

- Pay slip has been prepared and sent to the employees

Input factors / products

- Employee master data
- Employee contract

Output factors / products

- Pay slip
- Payment adjustments
- Pay slip data for accounting and reporting purposes

Segmentation, Validation and Notice

☐ value adding process
☐ strategic process
√ routine process

FSC
www.fsc.org
MIX
Papier | Fördert gute Waldnutzung
FSC® C083411

Kolibri 360 GmbH
Ferdinand-Jühlke-Straße 7
99095 Erfurt, Deutschland
produktsicherheit@kolibri360.de